Conversations with Practitioners

The Challenges of
Market-Led Microfinance

Guy Winship

Intermediate Technology Publications Ltd
trading as Practical Action Publishing
Schumacher Centre for Technology and Development
Bourton on Dunsmore, Rugby,
Warwickshire CV23 9QZ, UK
www.practicalactionpublishing.org

First published in 2007

ISBN 978 1 85339 623 6

Since 1974, Practical Action Publishing has published and disseminated
books and information in support of international development work
throughout the world. Practical Action Publishing (formerly ITDG
Publishing) is a trading name of Intermediate Technology Publications Ltd
(Company Reg. No. 1159018), the wholly owned publishing company of
Intermediate Technology Development Group Ltd (working name Practical
Action). Practical Action Publishing trades only in support of its parent
charity objectives and any profits are covenanted back to Practical Action
(Charity Reg. No. 247257, Group VAT Registration No. 880 9924 76).

Printed by Information Press, United Kingdom

Conversations with Practitioners

The Challenges of
Market-Led Microfinance

Contents

Abbreviations and Acronyms

CGAP – Consultative Group to Assist the Poor

DFID – Department for International Development

FINCA – Foundation for International Community Assistance

MESP – Micro Enterprise Support Programme

MFI – Microfinance Institution

MFRC – Micro Finance Regulatory Council

MIS – Management Information System

NGO – Non-Governmental Organization

OECD – Organization for Economic Co-operation and Development

PAR – Portfolio at Risk

PRA – Participatory Rural Appraisal

TEBA – The Employment Bureau of Africa

TPB – Tanzania Postal Bank

UMU – Uganda Microfinance Union

UNDP – United Nations Development Programme

Acknowledgements

This book has been a rewarding experience, and I hope offers something to everyone who reads it. The conversations I held with both practitioners and experts revealed their unflagging passion for microfinance and an inspiring commitment to fighting poverty, despite the considerable challenges they face. These dedicated practitioners have re-ignited my own belief in the need to provide savings, credit, and other financial services in poor communities.

Many thanks are extended to all the participants for generously giving their time; I know the conversational interviews often took place at busy moments and appreciate the great thought that the practitioners and experts put into their responses. Allowing me to take some licence with the transcripts to assist with the conversational flow of the book is also appreciated.

Many other people have aided in getting 'Conversations with Practitioners' to publication. The encouragement, support and patience of Graham Wright and the MicroSave team is much appreciated. Graham granted me total independence to develop and guide this project as I thought best, and therefore, any biases it contains are mine alone. Roseanne Petters invested significant time and effort in making sense from hours of often indistinguishable recordings; this book could not have been written without her dedication to, and good humour during the transcribing process. Recognition is given to Candace Nelson for the great editing job and to Shane Nichols, Edward Pearson and Jacqui Winship for the informal editing and other support. A special thank you to Jacqui for keeping the home fires burning while I was travelling and for enduring those late night telephone calls. The long discussions with microfinance colleagues in various countries contributed to the issues raised and questions and discussion; while there are simply too many of you to acknowledge individually, I do recognise the many microfinance practitioners trying their best to overcome the great misery of poverty.

These many efforts from around the globe have come together in one book that I hope will make a small contribution towards the huge goal to provide quality financial services to the millions of poor people who need them.

Last but not the least, the gracious and timely support of UNCDF/UNOPS towards publication of this book is gratefully acknowledged.

Guy Winship

CHAPTER 1

Introduction
The Shift to Market-Led
Microfinance

The term microfinance is quite simply, the provision of much-needed financial services to the poor. The terms most dominant in recent discussions of microfinance trace the fascinating history of its evolution – from the very early realizations that the poor, in fact, can repay loans, to the widespread endorsement of sustainable microfinance. With sustainability as a driving force, the industry homed in on the elements that were necessary for its achievement – growth, market pricing, quality portfolios, efficient systems, and professional management. While 'sustainability' has far from disappeared from our lexicon, new terms like 'transformation' and 'commercialization' capture the industry's forward movement towards full financial intermediation and access to local and international capital markets.

Most recently, the term 'market-led' has crept into conversations about microfinance. Encompassing the principles of sustainable and commercial microfinance, the concept of being 'market-led' adds a dimension too-long ignored: the clients. Rather than going to the market with that which they have to sell, market-led institutions are trying to provide what the market – i.e. poor clients – want. That these market-led institutions are investing in understanding and responding to market demand indicates another major shift in the way the business of microfinance is done.

Market-led microfinance exemplifies the convergence of business and social objectives. Increasingly, microfinance practitioners are realizing that in order to maintain market share *and* grow, their institutions must actively seek to determine and meet their clients' financial needs. They must invest in their relationship with clients through customer service, better delivery systems, and appropriate products. Institutions that offer a more diverse range of products tailored to real needs will have greater impact, leading to yet another case in which doing good is good business. And since bringing about improvements in the lives of the poor is the stated aim of most microfinance institutions, the poor themselves play a central role in the dialogue on how this is best achieved.

Presented as a set of conversations among practitioners, this book contains a set of edited interviews with the chief executive officers (CEOs) and product champions of some of the leading microfinance institutions in sub-Saharan Africa, as well as some of the leading thinkers and writers on commercial microfinance internationally. The conversations focus upon why and how microfinance institutions should and can become market-led institutions. With the support of MicroSave[1], these conversations were undertaken in 2003 and 2004 in part as a follow-on to a similar effort undertaken five years earlier. *Microfinance: Conversations with the Experts*[2] reflected the cutting-edge issues for the industry at that time, many of which remain relevant even today. The challenges that microfinance institutions are cu CRITICAL ISSUES rrently grappling with – market research, product development, client retention – are inherent in the relationship between the institution and its clients; a relationship that is emerging as a critical element in sustainable microfinance.

Conversations with Practitioners offers a decidedly institutional and anecdotal perspective on MFIs' attempts to become more client focused. Many of the interviews were held at two conferences co-ordinated by MicroSave, one near Johannesburg in South Africa in February 2003 and one in the Aberdare mountains of Kenya in October 2003. By offering a rare insight into the issues practitioners face and the practical strategies they are using, this book facilitates the sharing of current experiences and lessons learned. While the focus is on experiences in Africa, these relate to areas of microfinance practice that are universal in nature.

The need for a range of financial services

It is widely recognised today that poor people need – and can pay for – appropriate access to financial services at different times in their lives. Their needs for services and products vary depending upon a range of individual and environmental factors that include:
- personal desires (thrift, increased independence, entrepreneurial vision);
- stage of life (paying for children's education, marriage, raising a family);
- cultural influences (that govern expected expenditures on life cycle events, access to financial services);
- climate (exposure to drought, flooding, violent storms, etc.); and
- governmental factors (the degree to which governments assist in times of emergencies).

These factors that influence a person's need for financial services can be grouped into three categories:
- general life cycle events;
- investment opportunities; and
- the need to cope with unforeseen crises including illness and natural disasters.[3]

Such a diversity of life situations generates the need for a similar diversity of financial products, from savings and loans to insurance and money transfers.

Despite the obvious and compelling rationale for product diversity, its implications in terms of the need to identify and understand clients' needs have yet to be widely embraced by microfinance institutions. The industry is still dominated by a few loan products, regardless of potential demand for greater variation. Market-led microfinance, defined as the provision of client-focused and responsive financial services in an ever-changing market, is a new frontier. In order to understand how some microfinance institutions have reached this frontier, it is helpful to examine where they have come from.

Historical antecedents to market-led microfinance

Perhaps the primary reason behind the apparent lack of attention paid to identifying, and then meeting, client needs is the historical assumption that microfinance institutions are the major – if not the only – source of financial services within their targeted low-income communities. As the 'only game in town', microfinance institutions could subjugate clients' needs to their own growth and institutional performance, both cornerstones of sustainability. That growth has been facilitated by rapid replication of standardized operations essentially built around one or two credit products. With few other alternatives in the marketplace, robust client demand for these limited offerings provided little incentive to develop others. In addition, the use of donor funding, the inability to obtain regulatory approval to intermediate funds, and a fairly common focus on small business development (especially from American agencies) also contributed to this focus on the asset side of the balance sheet. Cost reduction, achieved through improvements in operational efficiency, management and risk assessment has been another important sustainability strategy. More often than has generally been acknowledged, institutions improved their financial sustainability by passing inefficiencies on to their poor clients through high interest rates and fees, a strategy that is

---

Expert Box 1.1

Success will come to those organizations that best determine the perceptions, needs, and wants of target markets, and satisfy them through the design, communication, pricing, and delivery of appropriate and competitively viable offerings.

From Philip Kotler and Alan R. Andreasen, *Strategic Marketing for Non-profit Organizations* (Revised Fourth Edition), Prentice Hall, 1996.

---

only possible in a context of minimal competition.

Yet, by the late 1990s, an important phenomena began to chip away at the monopolistic armour of microfinance. Clients were leaving credit programs in large numbers. In Africa, client retention rates were – and remain – as low as 40% per annum. That clients are voting with their feet is indicative of two very important developments exerting huge influence on the industry: first, existing clients are not satisfied with the services they have received; and secondly, they have someplace else to go to meet their financial needs. With more options available, clients are learning how to compare them and make their own choices. In those countries where competition has arrived, it is changing how the business of microfinance is conducted, as the conversations in this book will attest. Whatever the reasons for client turnover, low client retention rates negatively affect institutions' financial performance and compromise their ability to achieve sustainability. The need to compensate for the loss of existing clients (and loss of market share) with aggressive recruitment of new clients has multiple direct and indirect cost implications. Direct costs include those related to outreach and promotion, while indirect costs are associated mainly with a decreased ability to assess client risk. Both contribute to increasing difficulty in ensuring on-going cost recovery. One microfinance institution estimated, for example, that the costs of attracting a new client to a specific loan product were between 6 and 11 times higher than the costs of retaining an existing client.[4]

The need to attract and retain clients against a backdrop of growing competition engendered change within the microfinance industry. Some microfinance institutions began to focus on how to improve their delivery of existing products (an *internal* or *production focus*); others are concentrating on new ways to attract or retain customers to existing products (a *sales focus*).

The Production Focus – In the early days of microfinance, both international programs and local initiatives ascribed to the logic that tried and tested products from one country could well work in another. Products and delivery models that were successful in some parts of the world have commonly been replicated in whole or in part with little consideration for local economic, social, regulatory or institutional factors. Believing that lower costs and more efficient delivery were key to improved performance, these 'production-oriented' institutions focussed on the supply side of the operation. Cost-to-income, clients-to-credit officer, and operating expense ratios are some of the internal indicators they focussed their attention on. Rather than invest in tools to better understand client needs or in new product development, they remained focused on one or two loan products in order to achieve economies of scale with a minimalist 'one-size-fits-all' approach.

The Sales Approach – Despite the best attempts to improve internal systems and controls, the persistence of high levels of client turnover gradually motivated many MFIs to pay more attention to their relationship with clients. This initially resulted in more aggressive marketing and improved sales techniques. After all, they needed to continually bring in new clients to replace those who were leaving. They also made improvements in market assessment techniques in order to facilitate entry into new, untapped markets.

Microfinance institutions experimented with a range of sales methods, using both visible and non-visible strategies (the so-called 'above' and 'below the line' strategies). New resources were invested in enhancing institutional image through advertising, logos, coordinated company colours and spruced-up branch offices. Front-line staff was offered new training or re-training with courses such as "Managing Customer Relations" and "How to Sell Services". They learned that "the client is king". In many cases microfinance institutions interpreted this mantra as a mandate to improve client retention with stronger marketing, and indeed, in some instances client satisfaction improved as institutions did a better job of selling their products.

While the sales approach generally did not incorporate responding to clients' needs with a wider choice of products, it did assist in bringing the client back into the equation. The move to embrace sales led to an appreciation of the unique nature of the relationship between financial products and their consumers. Financial services are *intangible*; that they cannot be seen or touched or tasted means that a client's decision to purchase is heavily dependent upon personal experience, word of mouth, the institution's image and its reputation within the community. Direct selling, with sales being dependent on direct contact with clients is the only practical distribution channel for microfinance services, and it is therefore impossible to separate the service from the front-line staff selling or providing them. The importance of the personal touch that front-line staff provide in promoting and providing these services cannot be over emphasised. Microfinance institutions conscious of the need to cultivate clients with appropriate products and good service are now beginning to appreciate that the prevailing emphasis on productivity and cost containment puts pressure on staff to generate loans that may well be incompatible with an approach that truly places clients first.

Defining the new frontier: market-led microfinance

Thus, some of the leading microfinance institutions have started to fight back by – (re)focusing on clients. They are increasingly interested in a *client-centred* or *market-led* approach that investigates client needs on an on-going basis, and mobilises the entire institution to meet these needs to the greatest extent possible. The emergence of maret-led microfinance is the next phase of the move towards commercialisation, in which business principles are increasingly being harnessed to ensure that microfinance institutions can appropriately serve the needs of clients while at the same time improving their bottom line.

But what is market-led microfinance and how is it different from the microfinance the world has known to date? Market-led microfinance is the opposite of the previously dominant *supply-led* approach that was based on what the microfinance institution had to offer rather than what the client needed. Market-led microfinance places the clients' needs first and foremost. It conducts market research to determine these needs, identify gaps in the marketplace and assesses the competition. Such market intelligence serves as the foundation for a process of conceptualising, designing and testing the best product or products in response to identified needs. As a result, innovative products such as mechanisms to safely, cheaply and quickly transfer small amounts of money, and insurance products to help clients manage risk, are now appearing in the marketplace. But market-led microfinance is not only characterised by the number or diversity of products. In putting the client first, practitioners also embrace customer service and seek to minimize all the transaction costs that clients incur when accessing services.

Such practices are standard for any successful business. Indeed, a central and recurring theme espoused by industry leaders is that microfinance is a business enterprise like any other, albeit aimed at a poor and historically underserved clientele. Given increased competition, greater exposure to the formal financial sector, new regulatory requirements with specific prudential norms, and reductions in donor support, the environment facing microfinance institutions in many countries increasingly reflects the "regular" business sector. The framing of microfinance as a business is dramatically changing how products and services are designed and delivered since attracting and keeping clients – capturing market share – is key to commercial success. As in any other industry, practitioners of microfinance must view market share as the site of genuine competition. One hard lesson learnt in the more competitive microfinance markets of Uganda and South Africa is that market share is extremely difficult to regain once lost. Conversely, the retention of existing clients facilitates more rapid growth, further entrenching the leading institutions.

Beyond the business benefits of a client-centred approach is the *developmental* and *moral* obligation to provide products and services that address the stated aim of tackling poverty. The widespread use of donor (invariably OECD taxpayer) funds to support microfinance activities creates an imperative to maximise the impact of the products and services provided. Since these limited resources are the object of considerable competition among development sectors, there is a need to get the best use, and even leverage, from them. Microfinance institutions are usually established with specific social and business objectives – and their attendant fiduciary and legal responsibilities. Together these create the social, developmental and moral imperatives that should – over and above the operational factors provide the key motivating force for microfinance institutions to strive for a 'market-led' approach.

Attaining the dual goals of profitability and responsiveness to clients' often changing needs is not easy. For microfinance institutions to respond to the challenge of appropriate and/or multiple products, they need to fully understand the demand, and develop risk and return profiles of potential products and client groups. This is true both for individual products which need to be designed 'right' and for the institution, where aggregated risk can be reduced through a complementary product range. As the practitioners participating in the conversations make clear, the leading microfinance institutions invest significant resources to building full internal capacity while maintaining the flexibility required by an ever changing marketplace. Investments are required in all aspects of the business from the Management Information System to organizational structure, from governance to the use of appropriate costing tools, and from internal controls to staff training. In too many cases the lack of appropriate systems and related capacity limitations have reduced the ability of institutions to roll out client-led products. Only through serious efforts to overcome these internal limitations will microfinance institutions be able to genuinely serve the needs of their clients. Understanding that a focus on clients is key to keeping and expanding market share, the conversations with leading practitioners in this book ask: What have been the factors that have led these institutions to become increasingly market-led, to improve client satisfaction, to attain levels of client retention that are the envy of their peers? What internal and external obstacles have they faced and how have these been overcome? And overall, what has enabled these institutions to become successful?

As these questions are explored throughout these conversations, it is important to note that 'microfinance institutions' here refer to any institution that provides financial services to the poor, and includes for-profit and not-for-profit companies, formal regulated and non-formal unregulated financial institutions, Commercial and Post Banks, Credit Unions and finance companies. The conversations are organized into thematic chapters in which participants discuss their specific experiences in relation to the chapter theme. These themes range from the specific 'technologies' associated with market-led microfinance to the implications of this new frontier for organizational structure and governance.

While the book is built around the many interviews conducted with practitioners, each chapter contains 'expert boxes' which provide relevant comments from experts in microfinance who are not currently involved in managing a microfinance program. Chapter Two provides brief biographical sketches of each of the practitioners and the experts who participated in these 'conversations'.

Success for microfinance institutions is generally measured against three pillars: depth and breath of outreach, positive impact on the lives of clients and ongoing financial sustainability. These objectives are not always compatible, and the trade-offs between them provide a daily challenge for many microfinance practitioners, particularly as competition increases. If there is a single point to be offered from this collection of conversations it is that ¬while the attainment of business and social objectives clearly involves compromises – the only way to achieve these is through meeting the needs of clients.

Equity Building Society
The Evolution of a Market-led Approach

Established in 1984 as a registered building society, Equity Building Society is a leading microfinance lender in Kenya today. But this wasn't always the case. Initially, Equity mobilized customers through hard, one-on-one marketing, selling to family members and acquaintances. At the end of 1984 they had 1,000 customers. But by 1992, Equity was nearly insolvent with a deteriorating loan portfolio and a volatile deposit base. By December 1993, deposits were being used to meet operating expenses and its liquidity ratio stood at 5.8%, far below the required 20%. Yet, it was argued at the time that since there were no complaints from clients Equity should be given the chance to turn around.

According to Chief Operating Officer James Mwangi (formerly Finance Director) Equity Building Society's history spans four distinct phases starting from 1984. The first phase, from 1984-1993, used a "Product Concept Model". During this phase Equity believed that customers who needed mortgages would accept whatever was made available to them. Its reliance on a one-size-fits-all product led to losses and eventual depletion of the capital base of the institution.

Mwangi calls the second phase, from 1994 to 1998, the 'Sales Concept Model'. This phase was characterized by hard selling, promotion of the same products through sales campaigns where field staff went to open markets and other public meetings to sell the savings products in particular. The sales campaign, which was supported by leaflets, billboards, and other forms of advertising, led to some growth in deposits but proved extremely expensive, with a high cost-to-savings ratio, and consequently did not result in meaningful returns to investors.

From 1999-2001, Equity experienced the third phase that Mwangi refers to as the 'Societal Model'. Staff began to realize that customers did not appreciate a one-size¬fits-all product. The organization, with the support of development partners (UNDP, MESP, Swiss Contact) upgraded from manual to automated systems, improved efficiency, expanded from 8 to 12 branches, added 18 mobile units, increased banking hours, advertised on the local media, and perhaps most important, opened up communications with clients and among staff. The institution turned around during this phase and public confidence improved. The number of accounts and amount of deposits grew significantly.

Acknowledging growing competition from NGOs, banks that are downscaling, microfinance institutions that are up-scaling and Savings and Credit Cooperative Societies now licensed to open front office (branch and teller) services, Equity further embraced a client-led (or market-led) approach. It calls the current phase, begun in 2001, the 'Marketing Model'. This is characterized by a market-driven approach to product development and product refinement.

The product range has expanded to include a wide range of loan types, instant access savings accounts (there are no regular compulsory savings requirements), and fund transfer services. The product range now reflects not only a better understanding of the needs and wants of customers, but also a greater appreciation of the delivery costs associated with each product. Along with the revised and increased product range, operations have been developed to respond to the changing needs of customers and deliver quality service.

Equity credits this approach to its technical assistance partnership with MicroSave and other partners in such areas as training on market research and product costing as well as on-site visits and guidance in refining and developing new products that respond to demand. As a result, client retention rates have increased, and aggregate profitability has increased by over 400% since 2000. From 1995 to 2002, Equity's depositors grew from 28,000 to 132,000. From 2002 to 2004, they more than doubled again, from 132,000 to 308,000. By mid 2006, Equity had converted into a bank and was serving more than 750,000 customers.

Notes

1. A joint project of CGAP, DFID, Austria and UNDP, MicroSave promotes the market-led approach in microfinance. Further information can be found at www.MicroSave.org.
2. Charles Oberdorf (ed.), *Microfinance: Conversations with the Experts*, Accion and Calmeadow, 1999.
3. This has been well documented elsewhere – see for example the classic text by J.M. Keynes, *The General Theory of Employment, Interest and Money*, Macmillan, London, 1936, and Stuart Rutherford, *The Poor and Their Money*, Oxford University Press, 2000.
4. Based on (unpublished) work undertaken by the author, Uganda 2000-01.

CHAPTER 2

Meeting
The Practitioners, their Organizations and the Experts

The microfinance practitioners with whom conversations were undertaken are all either the CEOs or Operational Directors of leading microfinance institutions. They are senior and experienced practitioners, and a number of them have led their microfinance institution since its inception. A short introduction of each practitioner's microfinance institution is also provided, in some instances along with a reference to the institutional website.

The experts are generally non-practitioners, although the distinction is blurred in that writers and thinkers are drawn from past practitioners, and current practitioners have been drawn from the ranks of academics and policy advisors. In the book experts are quoted in 'expert boxes', with practitioners generally being quoted in the body of the text. It may be noted that the following biographies are updated only until the time of the discussions.

Graham Adie
Graham Adie is the Managing Director of Credit Indemnity, the microfinance division of African Bank Ltd in South Africa. Zimbabwe born, Graham is a qualified attorney, notary and conveyancer, who practiced for ten years in litigation and commercial work before joining Credit Indemnity in 1998. Graham lives in Howick, KwaZulu Natal, South Africa.

Credit Indemnity has been providing microfinance services for the people of South Africa since 1978 and currently operates over 100 branches countrywide. It has in excess of 135,000 customers, with over 70% doing repeat business with the institution. **Web address:** www.creditindemnity.co.za

Felistas Coutinho
Felistas Coutinho is the CEO of FINCA Tanzania in Dar es Salaam, having moved from FINCA Uganda in 1998. In her previous role as Financial Services Manager, Felistas oversaw the rapid expansion of the FINCA Tanzania financial services department to more than 23, 000 clients, a loan portfolio exceeding $1.6 million, a

portfolio at risk of 1%, and virtually no write-offs. Felistas is a Ugandan citizen who did her initial Bachelor's degree at Makerere University in Kampala. She has recently completed an MBA at the East and Southern Africa Management Institute in Tanzania.

FINCA Tanzania, an affiliate of the FINCA International network, is one of the leading microfinance institutions in Tanzania, delivering services through the Village Banking group lending methodology. FINCA Tanzania's working capital loans range from $30 to $3,000. Commencing operations in 1998, the program has grown to serve more than 27,000 self-employed businesswomen. FINCA Tanzania became a profitable financial institution generating an operating surplus one year ahead of schedule. The program is now preparing to become one of the first microfinance institutions to transform into a deposit-taking institution, diversify its product mix and introduce individual-based microleasing services. **Web address:** http://villagebanking.org

Craig Churchill
Craig Churchill joined the International Labour Organization's Social Finance Programme in 2001. Craig has more than a decade of microfinance experience in both developed and developing countries including Get Ahead Foundation in South Africa, ACCION International, the MicroFinance Network, and Calmeadow. In his current position, he focuses primarily on the role of financial services that the poor can use to manage risks and reduce their vulnerability, including microinsurance and emergency loans.

Gerhard Coetzee
Gerhard Coetzee is Director of the Finance and Enterprise group at ECIAfrica (Pty) Ltd, Johannesburg, South Africa. Gerhard was appointed as Secretary to the Presidential Commission on Access to Rural Financial Services in 1995 (Strauss Commission) in South Africa, and led one of the technical task teams. At the Development Bank of Southern Africa, where he worked from 1986 to 1998, he was responsible for policy work on development finance, rural finance and agricultural finance, and also worked on the operational side of the Bank. He is past Chair of Agricultural and Rural Finance at the University of Pretoria where he implemented the first post-graduate programme in agricultural and rural finance in South Africa. He joined ECIAfrica as a full time staff member in 2001 and still keeps a part-time appointment as Professor on the Rural and Agricultural Finance Programme at the University of Pretoria. He received his PhD from the University of Pretoria in 1998 and has published widely on all aspects of development finance as well as editing and writing two books on aspects of rural finance. He leads several teams investigating different aspects

of micro and rural finance in southern Africa, has served on the restructuring teams of several agricultural banks and also serves on boards of financial institutions. **Web address:** www.eciafrica.co.za

Monique Cohen

Monique Cohen is President of Microfinance Opportunities, an NGO she founded in 2002. A leading proponent of the market-led agenda for microfinance she is a recognized expert on the poor's use of financial services as well as market research and impact assessment for microfinance. Currently much of her work focuses on financial education for the poor and microinsurance. Dr. Cohen designed and led the AIMS project at USAID in Washington, where she served as Senior Technical Advisor in the Office of Microenterprise Development, 1994-2002. Monique has published extensively on microfinance and teaches at the University of Southern New Hampshire's Microenterprise Development Institute and the Microfinance Training Program in Boulder, Colorado. She is co¬author with Jennefer Sebstad of *Microfinance, Risk Management and Poverty* (1999) and *Reducing Vulnerability: the Demand for Microinsurance* (2001). **Web address:** www.microfinanceopportunities.org

David Cracknell

David Cracknell joined MicroSave in 2001, providing immensely valuable additional impetus to the programme. He manages MicroSave's Action Research Programme, which assists selected MFIs and commercial banks in Eastern and Southern Africa to move onto a market-led approach to microfinance. David has 10 years experience in microfinance, after a career in accountancy. He has experience in the design, monitoring, and evaluation of microfinance programmes, including networks and capacity building initiatives. He has a particular interest in client-focused product development and the institutional changes necessary to achieve this, as well as e-banking. David formerly worked in Bangladesh managing the Enterprise Development Programme for the United Kingdom's Department for International Development (DFID), which comprised microfinance and business development services. In Sri Lanka David was employed by a large Microfinance Institution.

MicroSave is a unique microfinance capacity-building project based in Kenya that promotes the development of a market-led and client-responsive approach. MicroSave is an industry leader in this area, and is contributing significantly to the global debate on the importance of broadening the boundaries of financial service provision to the poor. Further information on MicroSave can be found at the end of this book. **Web address:** http://www.microsave.org/

David Ferrand

David Ferrand has worked on pro-poor financial sector development and small to medium enterprise (SME) development since 1993. Before this he trained and worked as a banker. His experience included a period in Kenya as a lending manager dealing primarily with SMEs. David is currently financial sector specialist for DFID, East Africa, supporting DFID's programmes in Kenya, Uganda and Tanzania. Recent activities have been directed towards designing and establishing new programmes of support for financial sector in each of the three countries in the region. These programmes encompass and build on DFID's existing work in microfinance and SME finance, aiming to enhance the focus on pro-poor financial system development. His research work has been directed at SME development and the impact of the institutional environment on the development process.

Jenny Hoffmann

Jenny Hoffmann has been Managing Director of Teba Bank Ltd. from February 1999. Born in the UK but resident in South Africa since 1987, Jenny is a Chartered Accountant with an MBA and over 15 years experience in development finance. As Managing Director of Teba, Jenny led the organization's transformation from a savings fund trust to a full universal commercial bank with a continued focus on the low end of the retail banking market. She is a member of the Board of Banking Council in South Africa and has been a speaker at numerous microfinance conferences in South Africa and abroad. She is currently involved in developing a new Microfinance MBA at the University of Pretoria in South Africa.

Teba Bank Limited was transformed in July 2000 from a savings trust to a fully regulated micro finance bank operating in South Africa as well as making payments in the surrounding countries. The bank was originally created 25 years ago, to provide financial services for mineworkers and their dependents. However, over the last couple of years the bank has begun widening its market beyond the mining industry and now holds about 100,000 accounts unrelated to mineworkers. The basic savings account and transmission services have been expanded to include small loans, funeral insurance and fixed deposit products and the infrastructure has been updated with a new core banking system and wireless network, which allows all offices to operate on line. The last few years have also seen the introduction of new expertise, particularly in the areas of marketing and risk management. The bank will be expanding with a combination of new branches, alliances and the use of debit cards issued by agents from Point of Sales devices. **Web address:** www.tebabank. co.za

Martin Holtmann

Martin Holtman is the Lead Microfinance Specialist for CGAP. German born, Martin studied Economics and Business Administration in Trier, Dublin and at Harvard University before joining IPC and later becoming Managing Director. He has undertaken short term missions in a range of African, Latin American and Eastern European countries and played a key role in the design phase of the Russia Small Business Fund (RSBF), based in Moscow from 1995. He has also been responsible for additional institution building projects in Russia and Eastern Europe. In addition to extensive conference presentations Martin has also been a course instructor at the Microfinance Training Programme at the Economics Institute, University of Colorado. **Web address:** www.cgap.org

Imani Kajula

Imani Kajula has held a number of marketing and product development positions, and is currently head of marketing and product development at Tanzania Postal Bank. He lives in Dar es Salaam, Tanzania.

Tanzania Postal Bank (TPB) became operational on March 1, 1993, as a separate and autonomous entity from the former Tanzania Posts and Telecommunications Corporation. The Government of Tanzania is the major shareholder (43.5%). TPB is allowed to mobilize savings, provide banking services throughout Tanzania, accept deposits, administer special funds placed with the bank and to undertake any other functions performed by commercial banks except cheque clearance. The bank operates through four full-fledged branches and one annex soon to become a full branch, fifteen Regional Operating Units based in the regional headquarters and one district operating office in Dar es Salaam. The bank also operates 113 agencies based in post offices scattered throughout the country under agreement with Tanzania Posts Corporation. TPB has a large customer base that has increased over the years reaching over 1 million. **Web address:** www. africaonline.co.tz/tpbank

Alphonse Kihwele

Alphonse Kihwele has been involved with the management of Tanzania Postal Bank since 1992 and has been Chief Executive for the past six years. Before this, he worked as Principal Accountant and then Chief Manager of Tanzania Post and Telecommunications Corporation. From 2000 to 2003 he was also Chairman of the African Regional Group, World Savings Banks Institute (Belgium). Alphonse has a Bachelor's degree in economics from the University of East Africa. He lives in Dar es Salaam.

Fabian Kasi

Fabian Kasi is the Managing Director of FINCA Uganda, charged with overseeing all the operations in the country, including strategic planning. He was formerly the Finance and Administration manager for FINCA Uganda but left to take up the position of Chief Finance Officer for the Commercial Bank of Rwanda in 2001. Fabian is an accountant with an MBA from the University of Newcastle, Australia. He is a full member of the Association of Certified Public Accountants of Uganda and has also completed the Microfinance Training Program at the Economics Institute, University of Colorado. He lives in Kampala with his wife and three daughters.

FINCA Uganda was established in 1992 as FINCA International's first program in Africa. The program operates in a competitive environment with a small range of products. The product range is weighted heavily towards the Village Banking product, although MicroSave-Africa is providing assistance with the development of new products, notably a small group product called the Self-Employment Partnership (SEP) product. Linked to the SEP product, FINCA Uganda has been testing an open access savings product, with all SEP clients having the option of making both voluntary and compulsory savings deposits directly at a FINCA Uganda teller. A life, accident and disability insurance benefit underwritten by AIG Uganda (Ltd) is also offered to all clients automatically as part of their outstanding loan. Currently around 192,000 people are covered through this vehicle. Finally a health-care financing product in partnership with MicroCare Uganda was initiated on a test basis in April 2002. FINCA Uganda has grown to service approximately 45,000 active loan clients (99% of whom are women) in 29 of the 54 districts of Uganda with a staff of around 190. The average loan size for the village banking product is around US$120 and FINCA Uganda is clearly a poverty orientated microfinance institution. The program generally has a good repayment rate with the village banking product, and PAR>30 days is around 1.9%.

Michael McCord

Michael McCord is the President of The MicroInsurance Centre, an organization dedicated to creating partnerships to provide specially designed and managed insurance products to low-income markets around the world. He works extensively with several Action Research Associates in India, Kenya, Uganda, Ghana, and soon Peru to develop life and health microinsurance products. He has conducted numerous case studies covering all major models of microinsurance delivery, and has several microinsurance publications including the technical guide *Making Insurance Work for Microfinance*. Based on this work he trains donors, MFI managers, insurance supervisors, and others on the principles and management of microinsurance. He is also a key member of the CGAP Working Group on MicroInsurance, and recently co-wrote their *Preliminary Donor Guidelines for Supporting Microinsurance*. Additionally, Michael has considerable experience with new product development for microfinance and has trained and consulted in this area with MicroSave-Africa and Bank Academie International. Before this, he was FINCA International's Regional Director for Africa for two years, and FINCA Uganda's Chief Executive for five years. He has written on subjects as varied as pilot testing, rollout, and the feedback loop for microfinance institutions, MFI accounting and analysis, the function of laws, and extensively on microinsurance. **Web address:** www.microinsurancecentre.org

James Mwangi

James Mwangi is Finance and Operations Director of Equity Building Society in Kenya. He has been with Equity since 1994, following four years with Trade Bank Limited as Group Financial Controller. He has been the team leader in the transformation of Equity Building Society through a strategic mission drift from a technically insolvent mortgage provider, to the leading micro finance institution of choice in Kenya. He has a Bachelor of Commerce from the University of Nairobi and has participated in a number of prestigious international training courses and workshops as well as presenting numerous conference papers.

Equity Building Society (EBS) was founded in Kenya in 1984 with the purpose to pool resources of members for onward provision of mortgage facilities. The historic purpose of the organization has been to mobilize savings, term deposits and other funds for the efficient provision of loan facilities to the microfinance sector and to small and medium enterprises; to generate sufficient and sustainable profits in order to contribute to the members' welfare, and thereby to the national economy. The stated vision of EBS is "to be the preferred microfinance service provider contributing to the economic prosperity of Africa." The EBS mission is to "to mobilize resources and offer credit to maximize value and economically empower the Microfinance clients and other stakeholders by offering customer-focused quality financial services." As of March 2004, EBS had 76,205 micro-borrowers with an outstanding portfolio of US$ 29,066,667 and an average size loan of US$381 per loan. At the same date EBS also provided savings services to 308,000 clients with a total balance of US$53,333,333. **Web address:** www.ebsafrica.com

Marguerite Robinson

Marguerite Robinson is an internationally recognized expert on microfinance. She was educated at Harvard University and has a Ph.D in Anthropology. She served as Professor of Anthropology and Dean of the College of Arts and Sciences at Brandeis University before joining the Harvard Institute for International Development where she worked from 1978-2000. She is currently retired from Harvard and works as an independent consultant. Dr. Robinson has worked primarily in Asia, where she has conducted extensive fieldwork in rural and tribal areas and among the urban poor in India, Sri Lanka, and Indonesia. She served for many years as adviser to the Indonesian Ministry of Finance and to Bank Rakyat Indonesia (BRI) on the development of BRI's microbanking system now, the largest financially self-sufficient microfinance system in the world. She also works in other Asian countries and in Latin America and Africa, advising governments, banks, and donors, and is the author of many papers and books on development and microfinance. Her most recent work is a three-volume book, *The Microfinance Revolution*, published by the World Bank and Open Society Institute.

Charles Nalyaali

Charles Nalyaali is Chief Executive Officer and co-founder of the Uganda Microfinance Union. He previously worked for the Bank of Uganda in their commercial banking department. In addition to a commerce degree and an M.A. in Sustainable International Development from Brandeis University (Massachusetts, USA), James has completed a number of short courses in banking and finance and has presented and published papers on microfinance.

Uganda Microfinance Union (UMU) began in 1997 as an applied research project, and has quickly grown to be one of the leading microfinance organizations in Uganda. UMU offers financial services to micro-entrepreneurs and low-income people in rural, peri-urban and urban areas in Uganda. These services include several credit products, aimed mainly at micro-enterprises, several savings products, and most recently a money transfer service. In its six year life, UMU has recorded impressive results, including over 60,000 members, 150 percent operational sustainability and over 100% financial sustainability. UMU is currently registered as an NGO under the form of a company limited by guarantee. With the recent passage of the MDI Bill in Uganda, UMU now has the opportunity to convert itself into a formal financial institution supervised by the Bank of Uganda and licensed to take and on-lend savings from the public.

Stuart Rutherford

Stuart Rutherford is an independent researcher and consultant in financial services for the poor, especially in South and South-East Asia. He has a first class degree from Cambridge University and was based in Bangladesh from 1984 when he was Country Director of ActionAid's development programme. He devised and executed a system of offering savings and credit facilities to over 20,000 landless families in a remote southern district of the country, and set up the first-ever urban replication of the Grameen system. Stuart is the founder and Chairman of SafeSave, a financial services Co-operative which pioneers ultra-flexible savings and loans services for urban and rural poor in Bangladesh. He is a Board Member of ASA, a Bangladeshi NGO which is the world's fastest growing and most cost-effective microfinance institution for the poor. He runs Binimoy, a not-for-profit venture which promotes innovation in financial services for the poor and develops products. Stuart has published a book examining NGO involvement in microfinance in Bangladesh, two medium-length works on user-owned financial services, and several academic articles. He is a Visiting Research Fellow of the Institute for Development Policy and Management at the University of Manchester, UK. He currently lives in Japan.

Ernest Saina

Ernest Saina retired from his position as Chief Executive Officer with the Kenya Post Office Savings Bank in December 2003. In this position he formulated a restructuring proposal to transform the bank from a purely savings institution to one offering a full range of financial services to its market segment of small savers. Ernest has a B.Sc. degree in Agricultural and Resource Economics and over a span of 19 years worked in various positions in credit appraisal, supervision and administration and in management positions, gaining intimate knowledge of smallholder farming needs and requirements. In 1990 he became General Manager and Deputy Chief Executive, Kenya Co-operative Creameries and in 1993 he joined the Industrial Development Bank as Deputy Managing Director. He then worked as General Manager of Kenya Commercial Bank Ltd, before moving to the Kenya Post Office Savings Bank. He has served on a variety of Boards and Councils related to the banking industry in Kenya.

Kenya Post Office Savings Bank (KPOSB) was founded in 1910 as part of the National Post Office. In 1978 it was separated from the Post Office and became an independent institution. It is a state-owned company with no issued shares. KPOSB operates 24 branches of its own and rents space from the Post Office for 40 sub-branches. In addition, it has nationwide outlets in 316 post offices, along with 107 postal agents and one independent agent that operate on KPOSB's behalf. KPOSB is not permitted to lend, although it offers a visa credit card. It offers a current account, five other savings products and also operates a money transfer service with Western Union. KPOSB would like to begin lending, but has not succeeded in having its legislative prohibitions lifted. **Web address:** www.postbank.co.ke

Rodney Schuster

An Executive Director of UMU, Rodney Schuster has ten years of professional microfinance experience beginning with his work in the West African countries of Sierra Leone and Togo continuing through his founding and co-directing of the Uganda Microfinance Union. He has provided senior management leadership and technical assistance to over twelve microfinance institutions in more than 10 countries. His technical areas include: financial projection modelling, financial management, management information systems, product development and transformation planning. He has an M.A. in Sustainable International Development from Brandeis University (Massachusetts, USA), which is where he met Charles Nalyaali, the other co-founder of UMU.

Paul Segawa

Paul Segawa is Operations Manager of FINCA Uganda, in charge of six branch operations and the selling of micro loans and savings products in 29 districts. He has been with the organization since 1994, initially as an accountant. He has a Bachelor of Commerce degree from Makerere University in Kampala and has participated in a number of international microfinance courses, including the Microfinance Training Programme – Session II at the Economics Institute in Boulder, Colorado. Paul lives in Kampala.

Henry Sempangi

Henry Sempangi is the Senior Micro Finance Systems Training Officer for MicroSave. He has extensive experience in microfinance development in the specific areas of installing appropriate Management Information Systems including relevant internal controls. He also has a wealth of experience in finance systems development and implementation for NGOs having worked as an accountant and auditor for one of the international NGOs in Uganda for a period of four years. Henry has undertaken a number of short-term evaluation assignments in East and Southern Africa as well as Bangladesh and has provided valuable technical input especially on the programme design, costing and other finance related issues. He has experience in market research, strategic marketing and the evaluation of NGO microfinance programmes, training and institutional assessment. Henry is a member of the Association of Certified Chartered Accountants in the UK (ACCA) and he also holds a Bachelor of Commerce Degree in Accounting. He has taken on assignments for UNDP, DFID and CGAP.

Peter Simms

Peter Simms is General Manager of Sales and Marketing at Credit Indemnity. He has degrees in ecology and economics as well as eight years experience in Agricultural and Land use planning through University lecturing, Governmental advice services and private sector consulting. In addition, he has ten years experience in development banking and credit provision particularly in facilitating private sector-driven land reform and three years of experience in the provision of micro loans to the South African market as part of a publicly listed company.

Ben Steinberg

Ben Steinberg has over eight years experience managing microfinance programs in developing countries. As a Volunteer in Overseas Cooperative Assistance (VOCA) employee, he started up the Kazakhstan Community Loan Fund, the first licensed non-banking financial institution in Kazakhstan. Ben also started up FINCA Armenia, a program that served 2,000 micro-businesses and became financially sustainable within two years. More recently, he served as the managing director of FINCA Tanzania for nearly three years. During his three-year tenure, the program grew from 8,000 clients to more than 27,000 clients, generated an operating surplus one year ahead of schedule, and prepared the strategy for FINCA Tanzania's transformation into a deposit-taking institution. Ben has also worked as a self-employed small business consultant based out of Budapest, working in Hungary and Macedonia. He has a Master's Degree in Public Affairs focusing on Economics from the Woodrow Wilson School at Princeton University.

Guy Winship (author)

Guy Winship has more than 10 years' experience managing and consulting in microfinance. He was until recently Managing Director of FINCA Uganda – a leading African MFI with over 40,000 clients. He has worked on microfinance programs in a number of countries in Africa and Asia. Guy is now based in Australia filling both the role of Director of World Education Australia Limited and acting as the Microfinance Advisor for World Education Inc's Asia division.

World Education was founded in India in 1951 and incorporated in 1957 as a charitable institution in the USA. World Education is a non profit organization dedicated to improving the lives of the poor through economic and social development programs. It provides training and technical assistance in non-formal education for adults and children, with special emphasis on income generation, microfinance and small enterprise development, literacy education for the work place, environmental education, reproductive health, maternal and child health, HIV/AIDS education and refugee orientation. **Web address:** www.worlded.org

Graham Wright

Graham Wright designed and established the MicroSave programme and is currently the Programme Director. He has had a career of fifteen years of development experience underpinned by five years of experience in management consultancy, training and audit with a leading accounting firm in London and Vienna. He is a Chartered Accountant. Over the years, Graham has provided technical assistance to a variety of microfinance service organizations in Bangladesh, the Philippines and throughout Africa. He helped develop, test and implement a sustainable rural savings and credit program for BURO, Tangail, now an influential microfinance institution in Bangladesh. He provided long-term technical assistance to develop a rural finance system, using self-help 'Savings and Loan Groups' linked to strong cooperatives in a remote mountainous area of the Philippines. He has also worked on training, systems design, research and evaluation of both rural and urban financial services for a range of donors. Graham has authored over 25 papers, and most recently a book entitled *MicroFinance Systems: Designing Quality Financial Services for the Poor* (University Press Ltd, Dhaka and Zed Books, London, 2000). He is currently chair of the CGAP Savings Mobilization Working Group and a Research Associate at the Institute of Development Policy and Management, University of Manchester, UK.

CHAPTER 3

In Conversation
The Concept of 'Market-Led'

"For me 'market-led' usually means two related things, being the leader among your competitors and giving your client market what it wants. It means listening to the people who already get your services and also to those who might want them, and providing them the products and services they want."

Charles Nalyaali

What does market-led microfinance mean to you and what are the advantages or disadvantages of being market-led for your institution?

Michael McCord: Market-led microfinance means not just listening to clients, but probing them to speak, and acting on what they say. It means developing products for which we already know there is demand. It means selling products that people want. It means better institutional growth, and if done correctly, improved profitability.

Ben Steinberg: I see a market-led program as providing the product and services that the clients demand. Market-led product offerings are based on findings in market research. From those findings, the product attributes are developed and then the entire organization adjusts to ensure that the people, systems etc, deliver the product or service. This means, for example, that the organization must adjust its Information Technology (IT) system to meet the demands of the market, rather than the reverse when innovation is stifled because an IT system cannot handle a change.

In the end, it is critical to become market-led, particularly as the microfinance market becomes more competitive, with both NGOs and commercial banks. The disadvantage, in the short-run, is that an organization is likely to experience substantial up-front costs related to establishing and staffing a marketing function inside the organization, training staff, and conducting research. Once the product is developed, there may also be substantial costs in redesigning the IT system to accommodate a different

---

Expert Box 3.1: Listen to Clients
You have to recognize that you can listen to the voice of your clients, gather information and then organize it so that it is useful. I think that's the first step.
Monique Cohen

product. But in terms of the advantages, a market and client focus will improve overall performance. It is, in short, the only way to survive in a competitive market place.

Martin Holtmann: Yes, it's the same as in any other industry or with any other product – if there is no demand for what you have to offer you are not going to be successful in the business, and that's why I think that most of the very successful microfinance organizations at the very basic level respond to the needs of their clientele. Where there are no financial services then almost any kind of service will do as long as it is better than, say, the moneylender. But as the market becomes more sophisticated and the range of products expands, we providers need to move along, and that means doing things that earlier on we never did – such as structured market research, and tracking drop-out rates which no one worried about 5 or 10 years ago. At that time, there was such a huge unattended market in most countries that you could afford to lose customers because you could easily re-grow your customer base. So that is what I would call market-led development.

Charles Nalyaali: For me market-led usually means two related things, being the leader among your competitors and giving your clients what they want. It means listening to the people who already get your services as well as to those who might want them, and providing them the products and services they want. Then you must go back to them again and again; you might find that they actually need better customer service rather than new products. Then you try to feed that information back into the system and improve. So you are led by what others want and never rest or believe that what you offer is enough.

Expert Box 3.2: A Comprehensive View

For me, being market-led encompasses all of the following:

- *Viewing clients as clients, rather than as beneficiaries; realizing that clients vote with their feet when services are poor or unreliable.*
- *Basing service offerings on what clients demand, rather than on industry trends (i.e.: prioritising convenient/frequent savings opportunities and access over return).*
- *Not being afraid to charge a cost covering interest rate when the market will clearly bear it; not letting altruism stand in the way of a commercial service that can pay for itself without subsidy.*
- *Not subsidising services to the poorest from profits on services for the not-so-poor, but looking instead for innovative ways to make services for the poorest able to cover their costs.*
- *Looking for favourable behaviours; (a savings habit, rational loan-taking) and building products around local customs and systems.*
- *Hiring staff at the market rate; building an organization that is commercially minded rather than donor-oriented.*

Stuart Rutherford

James Mwangi: When we talk about having a market-led focus at Equity our understanding is that first the needs of the customer are identified, and those become the product and services that the company will provide and therefore dictate the delivery channels that the company will adopt. They both recognise the needs and the limitations of the customer. In a nutshell what we are really looking at are the customers' needs and wants packaged into products, and using the distribution channels that are most appropriate for the customer.

Rodney Schuster: For us at UMU, market-led microfinance means looking critically at the market on both the supply and demand side. On the supply side, what products, facilities, methodologies etc, are out there in the market? How, where, and why does UMU fit into the market? How do we price and design products on the basis of what others in the market are doing? On the demand side, what do clients want and how can UMU provide the services that clients want? UMU tries to be proactive rather than reactive. If we know a market is going in a certain direction, we try to institute changes in whatever area this change may be happening at our own pace rather than being forced by the market through, for example, high arrears or a loss of clients. At such a point, we would be forced to change and then may suffer more than not changing at all.

Despite widespread agreement about the importance of being client-focused and market-led, few MFIs are actually pursuing such an approach. Many do not have the capacity to do so. What then are the implications of not being market-led – whatever the reasons ¬especially as competition increases in the microfinance industry? Is this a case of "adapt or die"?

David Cracknell: Everyone knows – or should know – that from an institutional perspective you ignore your customers at your peril. We've already seen that customers at Tanzania postal bank and Kenya Postal Bank use unfriendly postal accounts very infrequently. But if you provide a service that is faster, quicker, easier and more flexible, people will use it appreciably more, and the transaction balances will be higher. At the Tanzania postal bank, about 40,000 customers who are using the DQA[5] product transact greater volumes of business than just over a million customers using the general postal account.So that says something.

Sustainability is generally a big part of what donors are paying for these days, so how do you become sustainable? You certainly become more profitable in the long run by pursuing a market-led agenda.

Graham Wright: Microfinance is one of the few remaining 'product-led' businesses in the world. Microfinance institutions that have developed products without careful attention to meeting customer needs will not survive – it is as simple as that. Performance and profitability are inexorably linked to a market-driven approach, which recognises there is more value in retaining customers than in attracting new customers who cost more.

Fabian Kasi: The advantage in this orientation is that once you are focused on customers, you gear your products and services towards meeting their needs, which builds customer satisfaction and loyalty, and leads to better repayment rates, and better performance. This is the only key to effective competition.

We have used several terms here – 'demand-side' and 'client-focus' – as opposed to 'supply-side', or 'product-focus'. Are the former synonymous with 'market-led' microfinance?

Steinberg: Yes. A market-led or demand-side focus will take microfinance institutions down new paths to many things, such as improved efficiency, better growth rates and stronger overall performance. The moves to commercialise institutions are much more likely when clients are getting what they have said they wanted. So I am sure that financial returns are better, and with increased competition these can be passed on in better prices, in lower interest rates and fees on loans, and on smaller margins between savings and loan rates. Better financial returns by the institutions that are market-led will drive increased competition and this will increase the levels of access in the communities we are working with. In the long run, the only way our institutions will be able to have significant impact on the lives of poor people, and to do this with as many poor people as possible, is to design appropriate products: to provide financial services that meet the needs and desires of the target market, and to provide these on a scale that increases cost efficiencies and related performance. So it all comes back to moving the industry to a focus on demand.

Expert Box 3.3: Client-led vs. 'Market-led'

For me 'client-led' is being responsive to your client with products, with services and how you deliver with them. 'Market-led' encompasses client-led, but in addition, it means responding to the markets you want to go for, being somewhat different in the market, and tracking the market share you are gaining or losing. This information may lead you to balance your clients' needs against those of your institution.

Monique Cohen

And the provision of sustainable and appropriate products and services to the poor is of course one of the main reasons for us to have this conversation…

Steinberg: Yes, the only way that the microfinance sector is going to attain financial sustainability, to be a truly competitive industry in the 'market' sense, to lower costs in the long run, is to be focussed on clients, to have a market-led approach.

Graham mentioned 'product-led' microfinance. What is the difference between a 'market-led' and a 'product-led' organization?

Peter Simms: It's not always an 'either/or' situation. Products are what you sell and what you know about. But you've got to trust that you understand the market and its perceptions of your product. It is all about the perception of the product. If it's been around for ever, clients may actually be quite comfortable with it, even though it might be a little bit awkward for them. You know markets are funny things; we cannot assume that they are simply governed by people making cold, rational decisions about who they go with. Familiarity and comfort motivate clients to stay with their existing service provider, even when another institution could meet their needs better. This is that intangible brand issue.

Expert Box 3.4: Commercial Microfinance

In the early 1980s, advocates of the financial systems approach to microfinance joined the principles of commercial finance to the growing knowledge of the microfinance market. Commercial microfinance has been developing rapidly ever since. By commercial microfinance, I mean the delivery of small-scale financial services, primarily credit and voluntary savings (but also including other products such as remittances, fund transfers, payments, and insurance). In its advanced form, commercial microfinance is provided by regulated, competing, financially self-sufficient institutions of different types. Some specialize in microfinance, while others serve a wide range of clients. Yet all serve low and lower-middle-income clients: those typically without access to the commercial banks and finance companies of their countries. Loans are financed by various combinations of voluntary savings from the public, commercial debt, equity investments, and retained earnings. Interest rate spreads permit institutional profits. Ongoing subsidies are no longer needed. The institutions' access to financial markets and public savings makes it possible for them to serve large numbers of low-income borrowers. Where competition has developed, efficiency and client service have typically improved. And industry standards are being developed. The extent to which commercial microfinance has developed in different countries varies greatly. But overall, unprecedented industry growth has occurred in the last decade.

Marguerite Robinson

Client service is another area that we haven't paid enough attention to. I think we as an institution have a pretty good client service, but we don't measure it. We don't look enough at where we can improve it. You know there is a lot of stuff you can do to improve your service, but sometimes this may not be enough. So branding, service levels, advertising and product information, and the way in which your own internal systems support the client delivery process, are all important aspects of being market-led, not simply whether the product is what you think the client wants.

What happens when clients' desires conflict with institutional needs? An obvious example is the client who wants a loan that she doesn't have to repay.

Paul Segawa: Yes, in fact, products appropriate to the needs of clients will already have a market making them easy to sell. The challenge surfaces when meeting a need in the manner that the market seeks is too expensive for the company, resulting in a price that may not be affordable for clients.

Schuster: Well, of course there has to be a balance between what the clients want and the services that can be provided or the institution will not be sustainable. But I think that as much as possible you try to meet client needs and then take those needs and try to blend them into your institutional needs. Generally the client needs should be first, and then institutional needs after. For example, if clients want a housing loan – you say "fine, let's work out how to price it"; once you decide on your price which meets your institutional needs, you look at the competition and then see how all three sort of mesh. You reach equilibrium between the three – what other players are doing, what clients want and what the institution needs to offer the product. This is sustainable, market-led microfinance.

Mwangi: Of course, sometimes it is very challenging because unless you are creative enough there is conflict between what the organization wants and what the customer wants. If the conflict is great you may be tempted to do nothing. But the trick is to be able to leap over the conflict between the organization's needs (the investors, the employees and the management) and those of the customers. One of the ways we have managed to resolve this is by being creative in generating the solution. For instance, at Equity, we changed from calculating interest on a declining balance to a flat rate on a monthly basis. Although the interest rate remains almost the same the customers were more satisfied. We found that clients don't always know what the service is costing them – they want prices that they understand and are able to compute themselves.

Market-led microfinance clearly implies multiple practices that are new to many MFIs – market research, establishing processes through which client input and feedback are fed back into the products and services offered, monitoring client satisfaction, etc. And as we discussed, these practices are not only associated with new product development, they need to be implemented on an ongoing basis. Can you say there is a single key ingredient in ensuring this is done?

Simms: The most central issue is the staff, and among staff, the management leadership is key, the chief executive is critical. However, a market-orientated CEO is a 'non-negative', that is, without one, the microfinance institution will never be market-led, even with one, the institution may still not reach this goal, as many other factors come into play.

Nalyaali: Well, Guy, I have heard you say that "management, management, and management" were the three most important issues at any microfinance institution, and I'd agree with you. The management and CEO are for me where the culture and values of an organization begin, where a company starts to build a client focus. The Board and management must constantly be checking to ensure that the institution is on the client-focused path, ensure the plans and budgets and strategy are in line with this, and get everything back on the path when someone strays from it.

Segawa: Management is critical, but no single factor is key to getting the institution to become market-led. A dedicated staff and the Board, low drop-out rates, and knowledge of customer needs are all key. I think also that staff and client incentives can play a role in developing a market-led orientation in an institution as they can orientate behaviours in a coordinated manner.

Management must not only lead the orientation towards a market-led approach but must also explicitly define those values both in writing and through action, ensuring that the necessary resources, systems and intra-organizational co-ordination are in place to move the entire institution in the direction of clients, in a cohesive manner. Do you agree with this?

Nalyaali: Of course the entire company, all departments and staff and the Board, must work together towards the goal of being a market-focused institution. Cohesion, as you say, is vital.

What is the connection between market-led microfinance and achieving the scale and outreach we need to make a real difference in fighting poverty?

Wright: The challenge of providing financial services to poor people is largely in doing so in the most cost-effective and efficient manner, in doing so sustainably, in ensuring the services provided are appropriate to the needs of the target market, and of course, doing all this for as many poor people as possible – getting to scale. Achieving much of this depends on MFIs understanding the needs and opportunities faced by the poor and the vulnerable non-poor, and using this knowledge to provide appropriate, high quality financial products. This will benefit both poor people and the institution. This is a market-led approach.

While market-led microfinance places a priority on responding to market demand, the supply side should not be forgotten. MFIs need to understand the whole marketplace including their own niche and how they compare to competitors.

In an increasingly competitive industry, adopting a market-led approach will be key to MFI survival. Ignore your clients at your peril!

Note
5. Domicile-Quick Savings Account product.

KEY POINT SUMMARY

- Market-led microfinance means:

  - using market research to understand market demand and design new products;
  - responding to market demand rather than selling clients the products that you have;
  - encouraging your clients to speak, listening to what they say, and using this information to improve your program; and
  - changing the organizational culture to put the client first.

- Market-led microfinance is usually synonymous with an approach that is commercial and sustainable in nature.

- In addition to refining existing products and developing new ones, market-led MFIs embrace customer service.

  - The advantages of a market-led approach include:
  - Higher rates of client retention
  - Diversified income sources
  - Diversified risks
  - Increased outreach
  - Improved financial performance, greater profitability and sustainability

- The disadvantages of adopting a market-led approach include significant ongoing investments in market research, staff training, IT development, and other areas.

- The leadership, including Board, CEO and management, has to embrace a market-led approach, and demonstrate to all that clients are the institution's priority.

CHAPTER 4

Knowing Your Market

"The market is becoming more competitive, so our challenge is that we have to find ways to meet clients' demands even in areas where our needs may diverge. The day is coming where if you don't meet the clients' needs, then the client will go somewhere else to get what they want."

Ben Steinberg

What is your approach to market research?

Charles Nalyaali: Right now we have a fully-fledged department of research and development which carries out market surveys on client satisfaction, client needs, their involvement with new products, what the market is and what is required. In addition to that, we do what we sometimes refer to as market intelligence – we go to the market and find who is doing what, who is not doing what, so really like positioning yourself. You have to position yourself in such a way that you'll be able to retain the existing clients, and at the same time be able to capture some new ones. We don't have it 100% yet, but I think we have made significant strides in this area.

Rodney Schuster: Our approach is sort of a standard "ask, listen, and respond". This is done in a variety of ways, including quantitative studies, qualitative focus groups, and also informal data collection simply through discussions with clients.

Ben Steinberg: FINCA Tanzania similarly collects regular information on client attitudes through client surveys to determine their priorities, likes

---

Expert Box 4.1: What Market Research Offers
Market research helps identify the nature and strength of market demand. It should enable you to understand people's financial preferences, including how and in what form financial services can best serve them. Market research can enable an institution to fine-tune its current delivery of services. The microfinance industry seems to believe that growth is never-ending, but questions about the degree of market saturation, and the level of consumer demand now and in the future are critical for planning service delivery and resource allocation. Many managers have no idea about their growth potential, and the degree of market saturation.

Monique Cohen

or dislikes. We are using the MicroSave market research program for both product enhancements and product innovation. The findings are then fed into an inter-departmental team with leadership from senior officers. I think our research has convinced me of the need for new product development. It has been very clearly signaled by our clients, and the research has also underscored the need to make our new products more flexible. For example, our clients want longer loan terms, they want grace periods, they want in some cases to pay interest only during the term and then to pay capital separately, and they want lower prices.

Jenny Hoffmann: Like UMU, we conduct a mixture of qualitative and quantitative research on issues such as attitudes about us, our products, loyalty, customer service, products and so on. Sometimes we use outside companies to conduct the quantitative research.

Paul Segawa: We initially send out our marketing officer to conduct research and he basically uses informal discussions. Then we structure issues on which we need feedback on some small questionnaire or table for clients.

Some of your responses indicate that market research has multiple goals – identifying client needs, assessing the competition and monitoring client satisfaction. You've described how you go about the first of these, let's move on to the next two. To what extent does competition from other financial service providers drive your motivation to be more market-led?

Michael McCord: The competition in the market and a desire to lead that market were the biggest environmental factors leading to a more market-led approach at FINCA Uganda during my time there. The objective of staying ahead of the competition was extremely powerful, and the best way we saw to do this was through market-led innovations. So, competition has played an important role in fostering greater responsiveness to clients. At the same time we know that if we are to lead the market, competitors will follow by picking up our new products. This enhances the institutionalisation of an innovative culture to always stay ahead of competitors.

Expert Box 4.2: Use Existing Data for Market Research
Although listening to clients is absolutely critical, I think management has to first value the information that loan officers already have about them, and find a way to better use it more effectively. If management can incorporate this information and process it in a structured way, the institution can begin to make a commitment to gather it in a relatively easy and low-cost way.

Monique Cohen

Fabian Kasi: We also have to be on the lookout for new developments in the market that we counter in various ways, either by doing what the others are doing, or trying to do things differently so that we stay ahead.

Segawa: Yes, it's currently the biggest drive for change in FINCA Uganda with the institution closely following what the competition is doing.

Schuster: UMU tries to always be more proactive rather than reactive. As one of the market leaders, we want to always stay ahead of the competition. This helps push us to be more proactive rather than rest upon our limited success.

Steinberg: Initially, FINCA Tanzania was a supply-driven organization and competition did not play a significant role. We're becoming more demand-driven because the market is growing more competitive. We have a high dropout rate of somewhere between 50 and 60%, so our challenge is to meet clients' demands even in areas where our needs may diverge. Competition has now become particularly intense in urban areas and FINCA Tanzania has had to reduce its pricing and introduce new products. We believe that we can increase our market share and profitability by successful market innovation. This is critical given the situation in Tanzania where we expect competition to play a growing role.

It seems that we all recognize that increasing competition has a number of implications for organizations operating in the sector – from the need to pursue niche marketing, to a greater focus on organizational and product branding, to mergers and acquisitions between microfinance institutions. How critical a component is competitor analysis for your institution?

Expert Box 4.3: Market Research for Product Development

Market Research is usually conducted to better understand the operating environment of the institution and to identify the needs of existing and potential clients. Market research for product development is a structured and incremental process that is generally approached as follows:

i. the research objectives outline the specific issues to be examined;

ii. a market research plan ensures that the research objective is met with either or both qualitative (such as focus group discussions and participatory rapid appraisal sessions) and quantitative (such as random sampling) techniques being used as appropriate;

iii. the results enable the product development team to outline a product concept, which is then subjected to relevant pricing and costing analysis;

iv. the concept is refined into a product prototype (occasionally subjected to additional quantitative research to further confirm marketability);

v. the prototype undergoes a pilot test which, if successful, can enable –

vi. roll-out of the fully market-tested product.

Graham Wright

James Mwangi: It is a big component because when you are developing products and services, you are of course comparing with your competitors, and their products.

Ernest Saina: Sometimes the other financial institutions in the market have very innovative or appropriate new products, or refine and further develop their existing products, and this can change the way in which your clients view your own products. Different banks can provide leadership of the market and with product development over time, so knowing what others are doing is, as you say, a critical component.

Schuster: We received some good ideas from seeing what some microfinance institutions were doing in other countries, and even in Uganda we got a few ideas from what others were doing.

Stuart Rutherford: The competition does influence perceptions about interest rates – the 'market' rate for microcredit in Bangladesh is around 25%–40%, whereas SafeSave is 36%–45%. Clients may find us expensive, but there is a good market for what we offer: reliability, daily collection, open passbook savings, and small, flexible loans. The standard Bangladesh microcredit model gives bigger loans and requires less savings collateral; occasionally clients who are loan-biased, or seeking high leverage will disapprove of our small loan sizes and high savings requirement; but generally clients appreciate our flexibility and the individual service SafeSave gives.

Steinberg: A few of our competitors are offering individual loan products. A key competitor is the National Microfinance Bank, which has 108 branches around the country, and if it gets its act together to really start developing microfinance products it will radically change the market. So in order to be competitive with them we also need to offer the kind of individual products a client needs. Our own clients are telling us that they want individual loans rather than the group product. Sometimes what the client might want we simply cannot provide outside of the branch offices. Some of our competitors offer individual loan products but then our clients know they are an hour, two hours from the branch, whereas we travel out to the village bank. But some clients are ready to move on to a more advanced loan product tailored more specifically to their needs even if it means they need to come into our offices, and we need to offer these services if we are to stop losing clients. We heard a lot of this anecdotally so we organized a market research team to go out and research what products clients wanted and what their interests were. Now we can design an individual loan product in line with what they want and within the parameters of what we can do. If we don't move on this it will be an advantage the competition has over us.

How do you know what your major competitors are up to?

Mwangi: You have to do a competitors' matrix, particularly when you are developing a product. It takes you through their pricing, their products, their tools and the channels that they use, so you need to really analyse them and from those analyses you are able to determine the threads that you have to take on board.

Segawa: I know that an MFI once sent one of their credit officers to a FINCA group acting as a new client to find out how we operated and what our materials were like and so on…a good idea really!

Nalyaali: We also ask our clients. When I talk to them, I find out why they are using UMU instead of another microfinance institution. This information is not only for how our products are doing, but also for how our products compare to others, or where we are not providing a service, and then we can decide if we want to move into that area or niche sector.

Once you have an idea of what the market wants and are trying to respond, how do you then monitor client satisfaction?

David Cracknell: I think an important customer satisfaction indicator is the percentage of people who come to you through word of mouth. This isn't an immediate indicator of customer satisfaction, it's an indicator of your image within the market place, which I think is critically impacted upon by your levels of customer service. There are also a number of proxy indicators, things like growth rates, dormancy rates, dropout rates – your monitoring systems should be set up to capture these. If you want to measure the quality of service, then things like focus group discussions with your customers are important. You've got a number of tools that can be used, such as service quality questionnaires. You are going to have to look at certain key variables such as cycle time, the total time it takes a person to access a particular service, whether that's a loan or whether that's time in a branch for service. You're going to have to look at the level of informal costs. This is something that many institutions don't do. And this is where some institutions fail quite badly. The typical one is, 'What does it take to open an account?' You

---

Expert Box 4.4: Simplify with In-house Market Research
One of my concerns is that some MFIs want to approach market research in a very formal manner, bringing in research experts to conduct large-scale quantitative surveys. I would like to see much more emphasis on in-house and informal data gathering techniques, particularly ones that do not create a lot of additional paperwork and generate inefficiencies. I would like to see larger MFIs create customer satisfaction officers whose only job is to learn what clients are concerned about, to respond to complaints, etc. In smaller organizations, this could be managed through a customer satisfaction committee that met every couple of weeks to fulfil the same function.

Craig Churchill

can walk into Equity Building Society and 20 minutes later walk out with your account. In some other institutions typically you'll be told to go back and get x, y, or z. You'll come back with this and then you'll be told that you've forgotten something that you weren't necessarily told about in the first place. So measuring key variables in terms of speed of service, the key points within the customer contact chain are very important for monitoring client satisfaction.

Segawa: We get feedback on this from focus group discussions and field staff talking to clients. But we also have a suggestion box and a customer satisfaction analysis tool has been developed to help us to analyse the comments collected through the box.

Hoffmann: We use complaints books at branches to collect this type of information.

Felistas Coutinho: We also have suggestion boxes and clients can write their requests there. The other way is through the staff – they bring you feedback and they bring up new ideas at meetings. We also try to do at least one focus group from each region about twice a year. But our dropout rate makes us concerned about client satisfaction. I guess it is a combination of a number of things. We are still in the process of changing to a market-driven institution; our selection of clients and our customer service levels are not as good as they should be when staff don't yet appreciate the value of the clients. But I think the other reason is just the nature of our clients ¬sometimes they need to rest. And the way we track our dropouts, resting clients are considered dropouts. Some of them are really small business people whose businesses are riskier, so you would expect a higher dropout from that level than the more stable businesses. It's just the nature of the business.

Steinberg: Adding to what Felistas has said, management also meets with clients, the staff report on a weekly and monthly basis. We organize quarterly client surveys to determine client satisfaction. We feel that we have a good handle on client issues, the challenge is for the institution to overcome its inertia to implement the changes we want to make quickly. The obstacles to doing this are financial, time, systems and so on.

Expert Box 4.5: Designing Market Research

The tools and techniques with which one conducts market research must be situation specific. The choice of research technique should take into account the ability of the people who will do the research, the research objective, the time and resources available, and what market research has been done in the past.

Monique Cohen

KEY POINT SUMMARY

- Market research serves multiple purposes: needs identification for product development, competition analysis and monitoring client satisfaction.

- Increasing competition is encouraging institutions to become more market-led.

- Institutions need to be proactive if they wish to stay ahead of the competition rather than follow in their wake.

- It is important to monitor what the competition is doing so that you can strategize appropriately – a competitors' matrix can assist with this.

- Product ranges may need to change and expand in order to compete effectively (e.g. individual as well as group lending).

- Market research can be both qualitative and quantitative in nature and includes activities such as surveys, focus groups, informal discussions and questionnaires.

- Organizations need to examine their operations both to maximize existing sources of data for market research purposes and to develop in-house research mechanisms.

- Monitoring client satisfaction with your institution is important. Methods include a suggestion box, a complaints book and feedback from frontline staff.

CHAPTER 5

The Product Development Process

"Following a strict product development process is not always that practical. In the hurly-burly or day-to-day practical issues of running a big company you can't always follow the full product development process, but cherry pick as needed based on your experience. But doing a pilot test of a new product is always necessary."

Graham Adie

How important is product development in your institution?

Stuart Rutherford: It is the heart of our operations at SafeSave. But this does not mean developing new products, such as insurance or leasing, so much as it means reviewing and refining existing ones. Operations are built around product design, so new systems have to be designed around new or revised products as well.

Rodney Schuster: Product development is extremely important to UMU. So important in fact, that we have a whole division dedicated to the practice. We believe that we must be responsive to our clients and the primary means of accomplishing this feat is through the innovation or refinement of UMU's product line. Good products at reasonable prices delivered in a customer-friendly manner is the definition for success. Innovation is one of the pillars of UMU's approach. Our thinking is always that things may be good now, but who's to say whether in 6 months or 9 months we'll not be behind? Someone once told me that with the way our system is set up we could probably dominate the market in another 3 or 4 years without changing. But that's not good enough. We want to dominate the market for ever – so let's change as we need to – be pro-active rather than reactive.

Expert Box 5.1: Test and Train

For all the talk about product development, I think most of it boils down to two primary issues: a well-designed and careful pilot test, and staff training. It is extremely important that MFIs work out the kinks in the design and the delivery system through a pilot test or even parallel pilots to compare alternative approaches before they introduce it throughout the organization. Staff need to understand the rationale for the product, as well as the related mechanics and policies. If staff do not believe in a product, if they aren't armed with effective answers to clients' questions, the product will not succeed.

Craig Churchill

If you think like this, then you have time for the systems, you have time for training, you have time for marketing as opposed to suddenly waking up to find every microfinance institution doing individual lending and picking all our clients. Being proactive does mean applying resources to marketing and market research and to all aspects of ensuring the institution is market oriented, and this can require significant investment, but the gain is always much greater than the costs. We believe that if we don't do this now we may have to do it three years from now and the risk of having to do it reactively is much greater than trying something now, failing and tweaking it until you get it right. Like now, for example, we are doing individual lending, but we're not under pressure. It's doing well and growing and by the time everyone else perfects it we will have it already perfected.

What percentage of the success at UMU do you believe can be explained by having the right product? Has the appropriateness of your products contributed significantly to UMU's success?

Schuster: I don't know. What if you have the right product and the wrong staff, or the right product and the wrong methodology? So I guess, like everything, it's a holistic thing. Certainly, having the right product is a big factor, but then again so are great staff, methodology, capital and a business plan. So it's not as simple as just having the right product. You could have a really great engine but no steering wheel. I think we would all admit that the engine is more important than the steering wheel, but if you don't have the steering wheel you can't drive. It's complex. And it's also the right product for the right market at the right time, so changes in the environment can also play a large role in your success.

Jenny Hoffmann: Yes, product development is an important component of our success, and cost-effective and reliable delivery channels may be even more important than product development, although this is also important to us because we feel that we are still playing catch-up with our competitors.

Ben Steinberg: We have also had to respond to the competition. For its first three years of operations, FINCA Tanzania only offered group loans. Competitive pressures increased from other group-based MFIs and client dropout was high – up to 60% on an annualized rate. Commercial banks also began entering the market with individual loan products, leaving group-based lenders vulnerable to losing their best clients. Finally our clients indicated that they needed a wider set of financial services to escape from poverty. Part of FINCA Tanzania's mission is to ensure clients' asset accumulation, not merely to increase their short-term profits through working capital loans; in order to increase the productivity of their businesses, they require a different type of investment. So FINCA Tanzania hired the necessary staff and made product development an institutional priority, focusing resources and key staff on the product development process. This was a major initiative within the organization.

What product development process does your organization follow?

Rutherford: For SafeSave, the product development process occurs in the following stages: Inception – recognition of an opportunity, or recognition that an existing product has unattractive features; Inspiration – a guess that a certain way of doing things will enable us to exploit that opportunity; Doodling – endless drafting and redrafting of likely combinations of product features; Research – discussion with clients, observation of staff, and review of

---

Expert Box 5.2: MicroSave's Product Development Process

The product development process needs to be structured and systematised in order to minimise the costs and risks of what can be an extremely complex task. I summarise MicroSave's product development process as follows:

Evaluation and preparation: Analyse the capacity of the institution to undertake the product development. Assemble a multi-disciplinary product development team, including a 'product champion' preferably drawn from senior operations management.

Market research: Define the research objective or issue. Extract and analyse secondary data. Analyse institution-based information, financial information/ client results from consultative groups, feedback from frontline staff, competitor analysis, and other sources. Plan and undertake the primary market research.

Concept/Prototype design: Define the initial product concept. Map out the operational logistics and processes, including MIS and personnel functions. Undertake cost analysis and revenue projections to complete initial financial analysis of the product. Determine and verify legal and regulatory compliance. Use this information together with client feedback, to refine the product concept into a product prototype in clear, concise, client language. Finalise the prototype for final qualitative prototype testing or pilot testing according to the risk/cost nature of the product.

Pilot testing: Define the objectives to be measured and monitored during the pilot test, primarily based on financial projections. Establish parameters of the pilot test through the pilot test protocol, including sample size, location, duration, and periodic evaluation dates. Prepare for the pilot test, including the procedures manuals, marketing materials, staff training, and installation and testing of systems. Monitor and evaluate the pilot test results. Complete a recommendation letter documenting the pilot test results, comparison with projections, lessons learned, finalised systems and operational procedure manuals, and the initial plans for the roll-out of the product.

Product launch and roll-out: Manage the transfer of the product prototype into the mainstream of the institution's operations. Define the objectives to be measured and monitored during roll-out based on financial projections. Establish parameters of roll-out through the roll-out protocol including schedule, location, branches, tracking, budget, and other implementation processes. Prepare for roll-out, finalise the procedures manuals, develop marketing materials, train staff. Monitor and evaluate pilot test results.

Graham Wright

trends in our database; Design – collaboration between chairman, technical advisor and senior staff. Junior staff do participate, but care has to be taken to ensure that their concepts of market demand are based on correct observations rather than prejudice; junior staff therefore contribute most at the start and at the end of the cycle at the start by alerting us to behaviour, and at the end by giving their views on proposed innovations or changes; Implementation – develop management and control systems along with product, and write a detailed set of rules all clients must have a copy of whether they can read it or not; Staff training – at the branch level; and finally Promotion -word of mouth and fieldworker individual direct promotion.

Martin Holtmann: When we arrived in Russia we were the first new player to provide real micro economic opportunities. We did a hell of a lot of research in several pilot cities to just identify the financial needs of the people there. How were they being addressed by the financial sector? Where was an obvious market niche for us to come in and provide something new?

We then scaled the product that was finally offered as a variant on best practice in other countries – typically the Latin-American model – which meant, individual-based lending as Russians didn't like to sit in groups very much. It meant payment schedules of equal installments because of the very unclear situation in Russia in terms of collateral and things like that. But then we incorporated some elements specifically for these clients. For instance we extended the loan ranges because Russian businesses are more capital intensive than those in other countries. And so we came up with our first set of products which we then put into the market – we tested them in three pilot cities and made some changes, including allowing, in certain exceptional cases, unstructured installment plans.

Then we expanded the scope of the program gradually to more and more towns and more and more banks. We had systematic reviews where we interviewed customers, and brought in outside experts. Sometimes you become a bit colour blind when you have dreamt up all these products yourself. I think, at least during the time I was involved with the program, this review process brought at least moderate changes to the product mix. We kept adding more products because our client base evolved. We were basically growing with the new companies, and so by the time these companies required, for example, money transfer services or longer-term loans for fixed investments, we just went along and we were lucky we had the means to do so. The partner banks were very interested in providing more and more additional services to those clients. So there was a sort of product design and review process, but it wasn't structured in the sense of having a department sitting there and only worrying about this or doing that and scheduling something every three to six months – it became more a 'do-it-as-you-need-it' process.

Imani Kajula: We have made it shorter. For instance, now we have a product idea that has huge potential and if we wait I am very sure the next day the market will take it. I know this project has got potential and it has proved to be successful, so why should we test? The only thing that I will do is a pilot implementation with a few branches and see how it works before going to other regions, but this means cutting some procedures that are supposed to be followed.

Expert Box 5.3: The "Aha" Factor

Two weeks ago I sat with TEBA for a whole three days after we had done a lot of research in the field; although our objective was to come up with one credit product, we came up with three eventually, because we reacted to the new information and knowledge. In that process, I realised that it's actually a hell of an effort to come from data in your hand to a product design. There is a sort of creative moment that you have to have – what Graham Wright calls the "aha" factor. But I think you can structure it in many ways. At the moment MicroSave uses this concept of core product, and I think that to help people we should expand that more. With TEBA we put the attributes aside and asked what the data said about each attribute and then the design. And I think it helps the jump, but it's still a creative jump.

Gerhard Coetzee

So do you think more or less structure in the product development process is called for?

Ben Steinberg: I'm much more confident that we are developing a process for product development that is holistic and that we will want to use in the future. It's been very good because a lot more staff are involved. Its been much more effective in transmitting to the rest of the management team and line staff what the objectives are, what the process is for new products to be developed, and I think, most importantly it has been much better in terms of structuring how the new product is going to be designed. There's market research, prototype development and product testing with the clients. I think that's been a very valuable process for us and we really weren't doing that in any structured fashion before.

I think the key benefit is that we will have a more client-driven product. I believe that the margin for error is less. In other words if we go through this process and we start pilot-testing something and it goes off track, it will be easier for us to get back on track. There's better risk management. If something isn't designed correctly, I believe that with this product design process we are going to have a much easier time in managing all the risks – like misunderstandings by staff and clients, or failure of our systems to handle the delivery – especially when we do roll-out.

Holtmann: Very often, when you are out there in the market you don't have that much time to go through three or four reviews. Sometimes you just have to take a leap of faith and, in fact, I think some of the leading lights in microfinance operations have good enough judgement to have a very good gut feeling of whether they are on the right road or not. What is important is to sense when something is going wrong. And for that reason I strongly believe in actually setting goal posts when you come up with any new product regardless of how you designed it, and checking your performance against them. That alone will tell you whether or not you are having the intended success. And then of course I need to be ready to go back and re-design when I see that the product just isn't working out.[6]

From my former IPC world we never had too much of a chance to do all we would have liked to do – we never sat down with customer questionnaires or whatever – we went into the market, we first looked at what the competitors were offering, including the money lenders in the absence of a formal sector or microfinance institutions; then you copy the good things that they are doing, and set the price of your product below what the others are charging. That alone will get you lots of clients. Typically within 6 or 8 months of lending you have already built a group of very committed people from the local economy – mainly loan officers who deal with the clients every day and who just know what is going on.

The important thing is to milk these people and channel their knowledge back to management which can be done in focus groups. I sometimes think that the best focus groups you can have are with those who are out in the trenches with the clients and provide that feedback. And they probably cost less than some of the other research methods, although I have a lot of respect for the systematic way that is proposed in the MicroSave toolkit. So I'm not saying don't do it that way, but I do have sympathies for those who say – "You know, we're under intense pressure here and every one of the workshops cost time".

Expert Box 5.4: The Tortoise or the Hare?
Competition can make product development much more difficult. On the one hand, the organization should be very methodological in pilot testing a new product; on the other hand, it wants to be the first one to the market with a new product.

Craig Churchill

Are other institutions also following the MicroSave process one hundred percent?

Paul Segawa: FINCA Uganda uses most of the product development process that MicroSave has outlined, and has adopted its pilot test protocol format. Some of the product development process MicroSave promotes is too time-consuming and costly for us.

Fabian Kasi: Yes, for us a product concept is developed through discussions with staff and customers and then it is refined before it is approved for testing by the Board. Piloting takes on average one year during which periodic refinements are done to the product profile and delivery system. If the pilot is successful, roll-out follows.

Alphonse Kiwhele: We have tried to follow the product development process, for example in terms of product development on the domicile quick accounts, the DQA, we followed that process.

Rodney Schuster: Our process is similar to MicroSave's in that we do market research, then propose a response to this research, hold planning sessions and focus groups to get input on the response both from staff and clients, pilot, review, sometimes a second pilot, and then roll-out.

Graham Adie: We didn't specifically follow that process, but we did do a pilot we ran it for four or five months. On an 18-month loan product, you should actually do a pilot for 18 months to ensure all aspects of the loan cycle have been tested, but this makes getting a product to market too lengthy, so we sent out a whole lot of questionnaires to different blocks of customers, different profiles of customers. We then gauged the response – to me it was a no-brainer. In the South African market if you are going to offer a longer term at a low rate, it's a winning product. Whether there'll be a big default on it is a different issue altogether. But whether the customers will like it is a no-brainer. But we don't want to do a pilot, because what if somebody else hears about it, they might beat us to it. We want to hit the ground running so we are not going to pilot – we are just going to go for it. Following a strict product development process is not always that practical. You know in the hurly-burly and day-to-day practical issues of running a big company you can't always follow the full product development process, but cherry pick as needed based on your experience. But doing a pilot test of a new product is always necessary.

Jenny Hoffmann: We also attempt to follow the MicroSave process closely, managed by our project office. But what we do at the moment is a bit of a mush. We try and fit the client checklist that they've got into our own project management methodology. Our project management methodology has been of great benefit so we think that we can put some of it in to make the entire process better. The project managers who are doing project or product development need to make sure that they've actually covered all the bases, which they might not be able to do without our project management system. When you rollout a new product you need to have thought about how it may impact on all stakeholders – internal and external – not just the client. There are a whole lot of other people and invariably we find we haven't gone through the process methodically and therefore some stakeholders can get left out. Following a structured process is critical.

In addition to market research, the two main emphases in our product development process are technological (usually an element of software development) and continuous risk assessment. We are still weak on financial projections and models since our costing capabilities remain rudimentary. However, this is one of our current priorities.

James, does Equity follow MicroSave's product development process, your own, or a hybrid?

James Mwangi: I think for the last three products we followed step-by-step the process they recommend. I think it is a very important process to follow. There is a lot of information that becomes available from the process and the marketing is good. There is a better understanding of the product so you are able to articulate it and sometimes there is a complete change from the initial perceptions. So I would back the product development process but I think there should be exceptions to get the product to market quicker. In a few instances where you are almost certain of the product you can make the pilot testing period shorter. You don't need to take all that time, almost a year, to get a product tested in these cases.

Ernest, How about Post Bank? Did it have a structured process for developing products in the past?

Ernest Saina: Well in a way it did through some research, going out there finding out what the customers needs were, or what the other banks have done, that we could replicate. One of the problems that we have been trying to overcome is insufficient communication in the bank. One department got deeply involved in this and they were doing everything, the development, the pilot and so forth, the operations, the finance, and other departments weren't aware of progress. So there is that experience one needs to overcome in the bank.

How do you think that the MicroSave process can be improved?

Steinberg: I think on a conceptual level the process is right on. In terms of the implementation we have found that we were developing an entirely new product line and there were some real challenges with that. When we started, there had to be a lot of discussion about the product; concurrently, we had to be training a development team to understand what the objectives of the product were, how the loan product would function, what some of the parameters for success might be. It's hard to design a product while at the same time you are training the staff to understand how the product is going to work.

Isn't this an investment in staff for future product development?

Steinberg: Oh absolutely. It's clearly an issue related to product development (now and in the future), but there was a lot of discussion trying to get people to understand where we were going with the product. We also tried to involve everyone, from senior management to IT and audit. We have really tried to draw in our people from all over the organization, to get communication throughout. They all have different perspectives, they all have different skills and skill levels, and to reach consensus, a lot of work had to be done both upfront and as we were developing the product. One of the advantages is that we were meeting every Monday morning for about two hours and we did that for quite a few months. We also had sub-committees that were working on smaller products, sub-projects that were contributing to the process. But my sense is that the team started to burn out on two-hour meetings every week, so I formed a sub-team to scrutinize the recommendations to date, go through them once again and make sure that they make sense. And then it came to finalizing the manuals for training, operations and client communication, which can clarify all those understandings. Once we had the manuals finalized, we could get the product up and running faster as everyone was on board. I must say that generally the extra work will pay off for us in the long run.

Where are you with the product right now? Pilot testing?

Steinberg: We're not quite ready for the pilot test. We are in the final stage of getting all the manuals and forms complete. I think we defined the product profile, had the profiles run by clients, then had them run by staff, then had comments from our advisory board and it was then run by our international head office at a conceptual level. Our next step is to take it to the International Board for final approval, and once that happens we can begin to do the pilot test and later the roll-out. We're looking at piloting the product over a period of at least 6 months, to about 350 to 400 clients, and we anticipate investing about $100,000 total in this pilot exercise.

Hopefully the cost of the design and pilot test saves money in the roll-out process. But given the significant investment you have made – $100,000 – couldn't one hypothesize that it might be verydifficult not to go forward with the product even if the pilot results look a bit suspect? Any comments on that?

Steinberg: In truth I believe the product is going to work and I believe that it is going to pay off big dividends. I'm not convinced that it's going to work the first time round; I think we're going to have to make some adjustments and we're going to have to learn, but at the end of the day we're going to have outsider insight, and if we can't deliver on the numbers, then the product is going to be cancelled and that will be taken out of our hands.

How will you know that the new product is contributing to the bottom line?

Steinberg: We'll track it. We have separate costing – in fact we have loan officers who are dedicated to the new product, so it will be much easier for us to track costs. We've also done some financial modelling, so we can always test some of the assumptions we made with the model.

What will you do differently if and when you start developing the next new product?

Steinberg: There are a few things. One, I'd like to get staff trained in the product development process so that they understand it better and so there is better internal support. I think it will make them more confident in the products that are developed.

The other thing is in terms of product change. I think there is a danger that in the middle of the process you can get bogged down, and again I would like to figure out how to lead the discussions and lead people through the process more effectively. As I said, we got everybody together – twelve or thirteen people sitting down for two hours every week – going through the process step by step. It was great in many respects, but on the other hand, it consumed a lot of time and I think people got bogged down, and we lost some momentum somewhere in the middle of the process. Maybe if we streamlined that it would deliver better results.

How long are you envisaging the pilot test to take and how will you gauge its success?

Steinberg: I think we are looking at a period of about six months. But I actually believe we are probably going to end up doing a two-phase pilot test. At the end of 6 months we are going to need to figure out what lessons we've learned, and I believe there are going to be quite a few. We'll have to make some changes and probably do a more thorough evaluation after 12 months.

Success would be good client demand for the product. Success would be a good level of loan dispersals, which would mean that clients could meet our criteria. It means that the clients are benefiting from the product and that they can and are willing to repay, and that we can separate those who can from those who can't.

We could also look at our direct costs, or the contribution to direct costs and we can track what our expectations are against the performance. And then we could also look at how we have managed risk through the process. Are there risks that we didn't anticipate? Did we thoroughly go through the design and actively anticipate everything?

How is the design for your product mix going forward strategically for the next five years?

Hoffmann: Well, the strategy has always been to keep it really simple and not have too many products – savings, loans, insurances, remittances – sending money and doing money transfers to rural areas mainly. Simplicity is the big issue. One of the very important things we did in our second-year business strategy was to introduce more flexibility in product development. At the moment we seem to be hamstrung by our MIS system. Every time we want to change an interest rate or the parameters of the product, we need new software development and we can't respond. This is one of several reasons why we've brought in a whole new banking system.

You've mentioned that earlier. I'm thinking about the debit card project you are working on – the project that gives clients a card linked to their savings or other account that they can use to withdraw from ATMs, or increasingly, at retail outlets. Are you going to be able to offer that to people who have low levels of literacy?

Hoffmann: Yes. We are still going to see what the take-up will be. I mean the big thing is how you communicate it. Because if you were to go to every person that you want to sell it to and sit down with them for half an hour to explain what it is, I know they would take it. If you had enough time to explain the product – even dealing with illiterate pensioners, they all would want it tomorrow, because they could see the economic benefits themselves and wouldn't fuss over a plastic piece of card or not. But marketing the product on a more mass basis is a problem. We always try to marry this kind of task with the radio, bringing those things together with lots of concentration. Leaflets are useless. Half of our clients can't read them very well and most just get thrown away. We also do everything in all the national languages, that's a given.

Charles, how many products did UMU develop last year? Was this too many or too few?

Nalyaali: Last year we developed basically two products. One was the individual loan and the other was the school fees loan. The individual lending was really a modification of what we call the MCC loan. MCC is short for Micro-Corporate Clients. I think this was enough new products for us to tackle in one year, not too many or too few when I look at our systems and people and clients.

Are you able to differentiate between your products?

Schuster: I think we are getting to the point now where we are having to acknowledge that with certain products there's an overlap, and to say well the new housing loan with its refinements may in fact be able to give better terms for businesses than the business loan does. So we have had to look at that and we've come up with designated features that differentiate our products. The key is to differentiate in a way that the client would never choose the housing product for business purposes, for example. If he would, then our business product isn't good enough.

When you develop a new product, is it indeed a new product, or is it a way of packaging or refining an existing one? And if so, are you not simply shifting clients to this product from another product – what some people call 'product cannibalism'?

> **Expert Box 5.5: Lending and Voluntary Savings**
> *Some fundamentally different principles underlie aspects of successful micro-lending on the one hand, and collecting voluntary savings from the public on the other hand. For example, microcredit institutions may choose to serve only poor clients. But regulated microfinance institutions that want to fund their microcredit portfolios substantially or entirely from voluntary savings must collect savings not just from the poor, but from a wide cross-section of clients. The main reason is that administering only large numbers of tiny voluntary savings accounts (that are designed to meet demand) results in prohibitive transaction costs for the institution. MFIs that successfully mobilize voluntary savings from large numbers of poor people do so by raising the average account size with larger accounts. Thus, financial intermediaries that serve many poor savers also collect savings from middle- and sometimes even high-income individuals, as well as from organizations, businesses, and institutions located near the MFIs' local outlets. This approach permits the MFI to meet local demand for savings services, to collect small savings from the poor, to use savings from all sources to finance an expanding micro-loan portfolio, and to maintain financial self-sufficiency. Such MFIs can mobilize savings profitably on a large scale and they can afford to meet demand from low-income savers with small accounts. Commercial microfinance in this regard then refers to profitable financial intermediation between borrowers with loans up to a cut-off point set by the institution and all locally available savers.*
>
> **Marguerite Robinson**

Nalyaali: I think it is a little bit of both. We have always had our loan product for loan terms ranging from one to six months. Then we increased this range to 12 months. The loan term for the new school fees loan is pre-determined according to semesters or school terms, so it is specifically controlled. It is a three month period; you cannot say 'please give it to me for six months'. So that makes it half a new product. But at the same time we are also giving it to our old clients. So it's not really like it's a new thing that has come from nowhere; rather, it is addressing the client needs and that is the focus. It came about when we realized that some of our clients were doing very well, but around school term time they begin either defaulting or getting hard up for money because they have to use working capital from the business to pay for the children to go to school. And then you know, it upsets the cash flow. We have just started this product, but I think it will be profitable because it is for people who are already good clients.

Ernest Saina: For us at the Post Bank I would say we have a wide range of products but I think that over time there has been some inertia, you know. We need to develop more of a structured package of products, of complementary products. We must get an appropriate product mix based on what our clients need. There should be cross-economies and other benefits in doing this both for us and for our clients. But as you say, we need to be careful not to 'cannibalize' products, although I do think that we will always have some clients who are attracted to the same product for different reasons, and so packaging the same product differently can also be an appropriate marketing strategy in some circumstances.

Expert Box 5.6: Cannibalization

Cannibalization refers to a situation in which an institution offers two very different products and one pulls clients away from the other. Several permutations are possible here. You still don't have the right product or you have two different types of clients. I think that you should investigate both possibilities before you come to a conclusion. But commercial banks do a lot of cross-selling and use existing clients to sell new products. Sometimes the first product dies and the second one goes on - it's a way of managing the product life-cycles of the whole product mix.

Gerhard Coetzee

James, how many products has Equity tested in the 10 years you have been with them?

Mwangi: We've only pilot-tested three products, one of which never went to roll-out. We dropped it. It was a product that combined both the credit and savings components. During the pilot test we found customers were getting confused as to whether it was a credit or a savings product. The other two have seen a lot of change – the pricing has changed and the structure of interest has changed significantly. The contractual savings product has also changed. The period of contract and the way it is packaged has changed significantly because the customers wanted it in a particular way. It's what makes sense to them.

Is there a trade-off in the investment in the product development process? How long should the process take?

Mwangi: This is one area that I think we should change the process of leading a product through to the client shouldn't be too long, although you must make sure everything is covered. I remember earlier last year we wanted to refine our product. We said we are not going to do any pilot testing, we are refining because we have heard the voice of the customer and it ended up we got it right, but you don't always get it right. So I think that there are times we need to have quick wins, and with quick wins, time is of the essence. You may choose not to go through the whole process, but you should be prepared to quickly monitor the product.

Segawa: There can be times when the full product development process does not need to be followed, particularly when you are making small refinements to an existing product. However, we have made errors in trying to cut corners...

and the lesson learnt is that the MFI needs to understand the benefits, costs, risks, and all the implications of short-circuiting the product development process.

Expert Box 5.7: How Long is Too Long?
Is an organization that takes two years to get a new product to market still client-led? My short answer? I can't see why not. I can't see why not at all. You can short-circuit the whole process, but if you want to do a complete design of a new product that will have an impact on your systems, it can take a long time. For TEBA, we allowed two and a half years from zero to hero. Two and a half years. We will tweak a bit quicker because two of the products are quick turnaround products. One product will be a longer turnaround time, which will take longer to pilot. You do not have to pilot a long turnaround time product through two or three cycles because the design is based on a lot of market information that we never had before so you have already hedged your risk there. Now you pilot and you're hedging your risks again because you're learning as you go along.

Gerhard Coetzee

Nalyaali: I'd say again...that we have not used all the steps MicroSave includes in its product development process when we updated our product, or developed the new school loan product. We are able to do that because we are continually discussing with and listening to clients. Only a very good understanding of your client's needs, your environment, your systems, all the risks, staff and your products' processes and needs can enable you to complete the product development process in a shorter time.

Of course, many people would say that a full pilot test is a risk management strategy. Do you have any comments on risk management and pilot testing, or other risk management areas?

Mwangi: Risk management is a major consideration during the pilot test, but there are parameters that you can play around with and it's during that time that you are able to determine the true cost and revenue drivers of the product. And so I see sometimes not necessarily risk management but truly identifying the sensitivity of the product – how elastic it is. Would you pull out some of the factors of the product? And those are the quick fixes that you eventually use once the product is in mass consumption. You'll have determined what data structure you can change and what impact it will have on profitability.

David Cracknell: I think that becoming a market-led institution changes and challenges the risk profile of that institution. You've got different specific cases – you've got credit institutions leading to savings, you've got savings institutions leading into credit. You've got the massive growth that typically accompanies moving towards market-led microfinance, you've got the difficulties, if you like, within the transformation process. So you've got tiers of challenges, and all of them imply risk.

Expert Box 5.8: The Many Faces of Risk

I'm an agriculturist and I think about risk in this way. If you operate in one geographic area, you have to loan in different sectors in that area, which could mean different clients, or you have different products in the same sector. Different products in the same sector means you still suffer from the risk associated with the sector. So, for me product mix where you are looking at the same clients – is no big deal in terms of risk management. You have to move with that product mix and combine it with the client mix, clients from different sectors, and then you improve. Obviously, geographic diversification is next; you can also achieve better risk here. An agriculturist has a wonderful way of thinking because you think about weather and climatic conditions et cetera which, in Africa, are critical factors for 30-80% of the population. A local businessman who actually serves the farmer two products, a medium-term loan for machinery and stitch bags, and a short-term one to buy the material for the bags, is still in the same sector and therefore, this product mix doesn't matter.

There are many types of risk – price risk, production risk, technology risk, the key staff risk, and I also always remember, the risks of political upheaval and social unrest. You have to consider all of them. Once again, if I was a practitioner sitting in a specific market, I would identify risk associated with my market; definitely price and weather risk, but also production, technological, and human resource risk factors, either key personnel or social unrest - acts of God kind of things. But regardless, you have to contextualise this 100%. Otherwise you can only have a generic, academic discussion about risk. It's meaningless unless your risk profile is contextually founded.

Gerhard Coetzee

Note

6. IPC is Internationale Projekt Consult, a German international consulting and financial services company specializing in development and management of microfinance institutions.

KEY POINT SUMMARY

- Success depends on good products at reasonable prices delivered in a customer-friendly manner.

- Staying ahead of the competition calls for innovation and responsiveness in developing market-led products.

- Products should be clearly differentiated.

- Even the right products need good infrastructure and a strong team to back them up if they are to succeed.

- Training staff to understand both the rationale for and the mechanics of the new or revised product is a key element of its success, because they are responsible for 'selling' the product to clients.

- The MicroSave product development process provides a useful structure and results in a more client-driven product with a lower risk profile at roll-out. Practitioners have both endorsed this process, and adapted it.

- Sometimes an organization may be confident enough of a new product to streamline the development process in order to get it to the market more quickly. This is a judgement call with associated risks.

- It may prove hard to drop a product by the time it reaches the pilot test given the significant investment associated with the product development process, but that investment is what helps an organization get the product right, making it far less likely to be abandoned.

- Institutions have to consider the impact of the new product on all stakeholders not just the client.

- New products often require technological advances in the institution.

- The effective communication and marketing of the new product is essential for its success.

CHAPTER 6

Pricing and Costing

"Pricing is an incredibly complex subject, but I think if you have a market that is well – serviced with a number of competitors, the pricing becomes less of an issue because the institutions will tend to have similar prices and drive them down over time."

Peter Simms

Why is pricing important for your institution?

Peter Simms: The price – in our case the interest rate alone – is where we generate our income, so it is incredibly important! Change the rate and our profits change…if only it were so easy! If our rates are too high then we will lose customers, and if too low we won't make a profit, so we keep a very careful eye on this side of the income statement, along with what pricing changes are happening among our competitors. Of course, price is also the major yardstick against which our clients compare us with other service providers, so it impacts on our competitiveness, and in turn, on our market share. But pricing can be complex. Sometimes, microfinance institutions 'buy' market share by taking a loss on clients in the early stages of the relationship. When the clients are 'locked in', you make a profit on them as they take larger loans, and as you know them better and can manage risk better, especially with those who seldom have a credit history. Knowing how long this takes, what the break-even points are, can all become complex.

In addition, cross-selling is an issue, one that I've discussed with you, where clients buy one product and because they are already using your institution and know you, they will return to you to access other services. So promotional pricing, product complementarity, the product mix, your branding, how you are perceived through the pricing, can all relate to the institution and product pricing policy.

Fabian Kasi: For FINCA, our pricing must be set to cover all direct and indirect costs, inflation, and provide us with a small margin. Our rates must be in line with our competitors on a value-for¬value basis, and so must be in line with the value that our customers believe we are providing them. But rates are not always so easy to compare, as products are not always exactly the same. In a competitive microfinance market like we find in Uganda, many microfinance institutions, even FINCA as one of the historic leaders, need to follow the market (and) keep their rates fairly similar to those of their competitors.

Here's a fairly straightforward question, but perhaps not one that – at least in my experience – many microfinance institutions are able to answer: Why is costing important?

Henry Sempangi: One of the key first steps in pricing is costing – to get to financial sustainability the institution has to cover its costs, and only by knowing what these are will the MFI be able to know if they are covering costs. But understanding costing is not only about being able to undertake better and more comprehensive pricing, it also enables you to analyse where your costs are coming from, and can enable cost efficiencies to be assessed, usually leading to better performance. Product costs and income need to be understood in relation to each other so profitability can be better understood. Some of our partners have costing systems, but not one microfinance institution we are working with had done a complete product costing exercise from start to finish. Although I have seen few microfinance institutions do so, costing and pricing can be a motivator for product refinement, or for looking into new product development possibilities.

Paul Segawa: Of course costing and pricing are critical, you have to have a good idea of these…but microfinance institutions with only one product, one loan product, may be an exception as they don't need to understand their costs. These institutions can just match overall income to total expenditure to ensure costs are covered. However, they are unlikely to be efficient, and will be in trouble as soon as they wish to introduce additional products.

So Paul, what impact has the shift towards being market-led had on your pricing and costing practices?

Segawa: So far, our move to follow a more market-led approach has had no significant impact on pricing and costing. FINCA Uganda has partly adopted the activity-based costing tool that CGAP developed, and MicroSave helped us with, but we have not yet adopted any new pricing tools. Pricing has to-date been based on competitor pricing. The only change in pricing at FINCA Uganda was made some time ago to help us attain operational self-sufficiency. And we haven't changed prices since then.

We see our price as transparent with everything packaged in one charge. However, from the discussions we've had with clients and the complaints they presented, the structuring of the price has been an issue. What we haven't resolved is that if we change the structure to fit what the industry is setting up, so the clients can fairly compare us with the competition, it might impact on yield to some extent. We may want to change the structure not by increasing the actual yield/interest rate but rather through the weighting of the portfolio changes or perhaps by differentiating prices according to a transparent client ranking or other method. That has been a stumbling block for us because operational expenses are still way higher and we haven't been able to reduce payroll costs as a proportion of the portfolio as yet.

So the key to competitive pricing and cost recovery is to find a way to

> **Expert Box 6.1: Costing by Allocation or Activity?**
> *The two main costing methods are:*
> 1. *The allocation-based costing method allocates each line in the income statement between the institution's financial products in accordance with a consistent logical "allocation" basis.*
> 2. *The activity-based costing (or ABC) method examines the direct costs of the processes of product delivery, such as loan application, loan disbursement, and loan recovery. Staff and other direct costs are allocated to the core product delivery processes on a logical basis, usually in relation to staff time spent on activities. Indirect staff and other costs are then classed in a general category. Core costs for the product delivery processes are then "driven" through to products on the basis of a logical cost driver, such as the number of loan applications. While this method enables the institution to better determine key process costs, which is not possible under the allocation-based method, ABC is significantly more complex and requires either a track record in implementing this method, or access to appropriate technical support.*
> **David Cracknell and Henry Sempangi**

increase the productivity of staff. Now my thinking is to find a way of reducing the amount of time staff spend on administration and other non- income-generating activities. That may mean for example, more clients within groups and, in my opinion, probably setting up a workable decentralized structure. If clients are going to get a better service, decisions need to be made much faster. We might have to pay more for rent, but the time savings – for field officers, managers and even messengers running up and down with cheques – will enable us to focus more time on the client. And that will push up the portfolio, and in turn, reduce the cost to portfolio, especially on village banking.

Rodney Schuster: There hasn't been a major shift for UMU as we have always tried to price our products according to market principles. Of course we know what our competitors' pricing is, but not always their pricing policies, nor what their cost structures are like…but we believe we are more efficient than most in Uganda. Again, as our institution has grown and become more sophisticated, pricing and costing have become more sophisticated and complex as well. However, the basic fundamentals of pricing products to be cost covering and competitive in the market has not changed.

Charles Nalyaali: Once the product is rolled out we actually don't adjust pricing very often, only if there is a change in the product or service delivery. Of course, in addition to making sure that we cover our operating costs, we also need to fund a reserve to cover things like portfolio loan losses, inflation and a small mark-up to keep us in business. And naturally we also compare with what the competition is charging for similar products.

Jenny Hoffmann: Our pricing is regularly compared to our competitors and adjusted where appropriate.

Stuart Rutherford: Loan prices have varied over time. From a low base they rose to meet the expense of delivering the service in the fashion clients best respond to (daily house visits). But recently, as our systems and productivity have improved, they have begun to fall again. Savings prices have fallen to ensure that better-off savers are not overpaid for their large deposits by worse-off borrowers. And we have invested in research into the cost implications of the allocation of staff time.

Ernest Saina: We determine our overall pricing to have enough returns to pay for the expenditures and retain funds for investment. And we have told our staff that we are aiming to get a 25% return on equity. If we can do that, then we are OK.

Graham Adie: In the last year to 18 months, we've introduced risk-based pricing, so the better you perform as a customer, the longer the loan term and the lower the interest rate you are going to get, as well as a bigger loan should you wish to apply for this. This is an incentive to the customers. For example our entry-level loan at the moment is a 4-month loan at 11.75% per month. It's a very expensive loan. But that's for entry-level guys. Once they've been on our system for 6 months, they will be allocated a profile and if they have a good profile because they have paid on time, they can become a diamond or platinum client, qualifying for an 18 month loan at 4.25% a month. I think that the technology and thinking are in place to reward people. Certainly as far as I am aware in South Africa, we are the only guys in the industry that price for risk, or differentiate price based on risk. I don't think anybody else does. In South Africa, switching between institutions is quite easy, and a lot of people have different loans with different institutions. In the past we gave short-term loans to clients who then got a long-term loan from somebody else. We are now trying to offer all in one house, which should assist us in our retention.

Simms: Actually, pricing is an incredibly complex subject but I think if you have a market that is well-serviced with a number of competitors, the pricing becomes less of an issue because competing institutions will tend to have similar prices and drive down the price over time. But I don't think clients understand the price of financial products properly; in South Africa the competing institutions are very deliberate about making it as difficult as they can. It's very, very difficult to compare apples with apples. The main commercial banks, for example, make 60% of their revenue from fees – transaction fees, administration fees, commissions, whatever. That's a significant portion of their income.

You don't think that clients are going to remember this? I find that financial institutions in general are not the most transparent when it

comes to the fees they charge; when prices include a mix of interest and fees it can be difficult for anyone, even me, to know what the bank is charging.

Simms: I'm sure that's true – I think clients notice if rates get raised or are significantly higher than others. What I am saying is that the pricing at the start was not about risk. It was about super profits here in South Africa. With a market that had had no access to credit you could make super profits. But this has changed as competition has grown and risks have been factored in.

How elastic is demand? Would your market share increase proportionally more or less if you dropped your pricing?

Simms: We believe that if we went and significantly dropped our prices say by 40%, we would initially get less revenue but that in time we would more than recoup these revenues and secure a significant market share, purely on price. Of course, we'd need to be sure of the implications, so we'd probably only drop prices slowly. And, one also wants to raise market share with additional products.

Some people have argued that the price sensitivity of many microfinance loan and saving products is fairly low, with client demand being somewhat unaffected by price. But this elasticity no doubt differs from country to country and from institution to institution.

Ben Steinberg: Yes, Tanzania for example is generally so under-banked, especially with individual lending products, that at this point price isn't going to have a big impact, and so elasticity is not going to be high. However in certain areas, especially with our group-based products, the competition has been tough and we recognized that we had to drop our prices to become more competitive. In the last two years, FINCA Tanzania has reduced its interest rate twice on its standard group loan product.

For new product development, we are aware that we need to carefully balance several issues. First, we have to ensure that new products are not going to lead to a cannibalization of our existing products on a price basis. Second, we need to price so that we are competitive with other lending organizations. In this case, our primary competitors are commercial banks. The issue is not easy to balance. In the end, we have recognized that we have to be competitive with market rates and that those are going to drive our product costing/pricing if the new products are to be successful.

How many products does FINCA Tanzania have now in total?

Felistas Coutinho: The village banking product, the micro-leasing product, the progressive loan (smaller than village banking), and we are also going to test what we call urban village banking, a more flexible version. In addition, we've made the village banking product much more flexible.

So that would be four products, all loan products. Do you know the contribution of each of those products to your bottom line?

Felistas Coutinho: The micro-leasing and urban village banking are just beginning, and as new products, we have only estimated their contribution. So I wouldn't know exactly. The progressive loans are also just beginning. We haven't even reached break-even point. But what I am seeing is that the smaller groups take less time to monitor, but the loan capital is similar to the village bank so they will be more profitable. We don't really have any fixed pricing policy. I guess we just started offering the product at a high price – like 5% – and hoped that it would contribute something. Then competition forced us to push it down. Maybe this price is competitive, but it is still higher than everybody else's.

What happens if it costs you more to deliver the product than you are getting paid for that product?

Coutinho: That's happening in some places and I think we need to look at it because in the rural areas where we service loans with motorbikes it is very costly. We are breaking even because the cheaper loans in Dar es Salaam are subsidizing the more expensive rural loans.

After covering costs, is there any internally driven requirement for margin for FINCA Tanzania?

Steinberg: At this point we have some financial projections that we want to realize, but my main goal in the first six months of our pilot is to answer questions can we make good loans and get retainers or leases? If we learn how to do that, even at a loss, the experience and confidence we gain is going to allow us to re-design the process so that it can become more price competitive. So for me, during the pilot phase the pricing is less critical than it will be later. The first priority is to determine if we can make good loans.

I believe that to do an entirely different kind of loan product in the Tanzanian environment, where many other people have failed, we are going to have to give ourselves a little bit of time to learn the process. If we achieve portfolio quality and fall short on profitability, we can re-design the process and figure out how to cut costs – I'm 100% confident about that. If we develop this product and we look at the future income stream that comes from it, it won't matter in the long term if we lose money in the first six months. Longer term, yes, we have to be worried about the cost of providing the service.

Charles, are UMU's new products profitable? And how do you know this?

Nalyaali: Yes. The charges and the interest rate for the individual product are the same as for the group product. But you are giving out larger amounts of money, so the administrative and monetary costs are lower, and therefore you assume that you are making a little bit more money. We have done pricing and costing of our products, and we are profitable, but we do need to do more work in these areas, particularly on the costing side.

And do you charge effective interest rates and quote repayments based on declining balances?

Nalyaali: Yes. Our clients actually would rather work with us because we tell them everything as opposed to those who quote the nominal interest rate without specifying the other charges. We tell them right from the start. Some may not understand interest rates properly, but as a matter of principle we have to disclose, and when we do, those who have understood will tell the others.

Institutions appear to have a difficult time apportioning costs to products. How does the Postal Bank approach this?

Alphonse Kiwhele: We haven't tracked the costs exactly by product. That is a problem I think, a big problem. And that is the direction where we need to grow. Currently we have people who are handling products that are not even issued by the bank, like the Western Union transfers that we do. Establishing the exact costs for this alone is difficult. You can try to apportion the cost in terms of the people who are working on it, but the fact that some staff handle this product very seldom makes it difficult to work out exact costs.

James, when does Equity do their costing on a new product? Can you explain how Equity manages its costing? I know you use an allocation basis rather than an activity basis and it would be interesting to hear your take on that.

James Mwangi: We do it initially during the construction of the product. When we are developing the product we do the costing analysis of where we are leading to, and refine it when the product is rolled-out. We use allocation-based costing because it is much more straightforward, and we already have the necessary skills and experience in place. I am not a strong believer in the activity-based method because of the time it consumes. I find it particularly hard to maintain time sheets; everybody has some extra time on Saturdays, so how do you discern the days? And can you just plainly assume that clients were doing withdrawals and deposits or were they seeking some information that took time but involved no transactions? Although MicroSave would like us to move to an activity-based costing, we have no interest whatsoever.

So the allocation-based costing method has worked for you?

Mwangi: It has worked. It has made the Bank extremely profitable because particularly with the savings product we have managed to change quite a number of parameters and I think that is what is currently driving the profitability of the bank. Understanding the cost drivers and the revenue drivers and to what extent you can play with each of them has been absolutely important for us.

I often tell people that costing is as much an art as a science! Knowing where the greater portion of the costs – are you call them cost drivers – means you can focus on those areas to reduce costs, and then move to the next priority area when you've got the first sorted out. Would you agree that having the costs exactly right is not as important as knowing where the costs lie relative to one another?

Mwangi: Yes, this is right in part. The second issue is that you must know the sensitivity impacts of whatever you are doing. Some costs may not be substantial in and of themselves, but if you imbalance them, they can affect the whole organization. A small cost saving may produce a related effect that offsets those savings. You need to understand and analyse both the absolute costs and their impact – the costs associated with the changes produced by the original expenditures. Once you take a particular costing then you see the absolute figures at the end of the month and the sensitivity is something easy to identify. For Equity I think we may not have made the effort to make the figures 100% accurate from 95%, as it is not worthwhile. Costing becomes even more complex as you get more products.

But at the end of the day, you are right – costing is often more of an art than a science. While the process involves some objectivity, it includes a lot of subjectivity as well; no two people are likely to allocate the cost in the same way.

From our discussions would you agree that you have made a number of assumptions in your costing, especially early in the process?

Mwangi: Exactly. Because you don't want to just start pilot testing a product giving you negative results in terms of profitability and wait until the pilot process produces actual data to test the profitability of the product. However, there are still some things that may not be adequate because you are not dealing with real output for the product, so eventually once you roll the product you continue monitoring it. For Equity at the moment, we are doing costing through cost allocation twice in a year to monitor the product.

KEY POINT SUMMARY

- Although pricing is affected by many factors such as competition, self-sufficiency requirements, overhead and cost apportioning, competition is emerging as the primary one.

- Competition in the market tends to level prices out at a lower rate.

- As competition increases, so does sensitivity to price.

- Prices among competitors are difficult to compare because they are structured differently, and thus, clients cannot compare like with like.

- Price transparency and fairness are likely to pay off in market share.

- With only one loan product, MFIs have not needed to carry out product cost analyses. However, as practitioners diversify their products in response to the market, they need to develop a better understanding of how each product affects the bottom line.

- Proper costing will lead to better performance because it helps institutions to price products to cover costs, identify their most profitable products, understand their 'cost drivers' and identify those areas in which they can achieve greater efficiencies.

- When launching a new product, some practitioners prefer to focus on getting the product right first and adjust its pricing later.

- There is a difference of opinion regarding whether it is better to apportion costs on an allocation or an activity basis.

- Costing can be more of an art than a science as there is always an element of subjectivity.

CHAPTER 7

Client Satisfaction

"The one thing that perhaps is not appreciated enough in the microfinance industry is that clients and customers act on perception, they don't act on the basis of having done two months' research to work out where they should get their loan from or where they should put their deposit."

David Cracknell

Why is client satisfaction important?

Graham Wright: Quite simply, institutions that do not put client satisfaction first and foremost will invariably be driven out of business by the MFIs that do. The high drop-out rates currently plaguing many microfinance institutions raise costs, lower efficiency and undermine financial performance. Clients leave because they are not receiving services that warrant the social and financial costs involved, or they have identified a better alternative. There are many reasons for their dissatisfaction, but drop-out analysis invariably points to inappropriately designed products, the result of replicating methodologies and product models taken from foreign countries without reference to the social, cultural and economic environment into which these are being imported. The absence of competition has served as a disincentive to undertaking appropriate market research, resulting in a poor understanding of the market. Furthermore, many MFIs don't understand their cost structures, which means that they don't fully understand the implications of low levels of client satisfaction and related high drop-out rates.

But how do you know if your clients are satisfied with the service you offer? How do you access this information?

Ben Steinberg: We've done surveys and focus group discussions and we've established a marketing office, staffed by three full-time people right now, one from the States and two in Dar es Salaam. We sent a market research team comprised of student interns, out to interview our clients, and collected a lot of information from that. When we did our first evaluation of the progressive loans, part of the evaluation checked client satisfaction; overwhelmingly the clients said they liked the progressive loan more than the village banking. In addition I feel that when the supervisors go out, they are talking a lot to clients and feeding this back to us.

Graham Adie: The main way that we have done it in recent years is through focus groups – externally-run focus groups because when we ran them ourselves, I don't think we got honest opinions.

You have mentioned focus groups, surveys, market research – all ways of learning how clients perceive the program and its products. How do you communicate with your clients to both promote and monitor their satisfaction?

Stuart Rutherford: We communicate with the clients via the daily meeting with the collector and occasional meetings with the branch manager, backing that relationship up with written product rules. Monitoring is done by the chairman, technical advisor and senior management through direct interaction with staff and clients, as one would expect. We do not generally survey or commission outside research, although we are now considering commissioning a client satisfaction and poverty level study, which would best be done by outsiders.

We all know that many microfinance institutions have low client retention levels. Aren't high drop-out rates an indicator of client dissatisfaction, of microfinance institutions not meeting client needs?

Steinberg: Absolutely. High retention rates are a key indicator of satisfaction; if they are low, this is likely to mean that the institution is not meeting client needs and does not have a market orientation. But practitioners deal daily with operational issues; the great many institutional challenges they face are probably the key reasons we as an industry have focused on the supply side, what you had called 'product-led microfinance', rather than the demand side – as characterized by finding out what clients want and responding with appropriate products that have been tested, competitively priced, communicated and delivered where and when clients want.

Rodney I know your retention rate is about 80 – 90%. In the East African context this is really good.[7] How does UMU achieve this?

Rodney Schuster: Good products at reasonable prices delivered in a customer-friendly manner. That's how we find new business, that's how we retain clients, and that is how we reduce delinquency.

You make it sound simple, but many organizations do have real problems with retention.

Jenny Hoffmann: At TEBA we try to retain existing clients by being aware of their views on an ongoing basis through the work of our front office people, by designing new products to meet their needs and continuing to improve customer service. We manage client delinquency through rapid follow-up of arrears by dedicated staff. However, one area we are not yet following up on is dormant accounts, to discover the reasons for this.

Several of you have mentioned customer service as a key part of your strategy to improve client satisfaction and retention. What do you mean by 'customer service'?

David Cracknell: Customer service is a focus. Marketing and the other areas are disciplines. Customer service may involve elements of different disciplines, but it is a way of looking at your organization, including marketing, costs, efficiency and delivery. Drawing from all these disciplines, customer service literally focuses on the output the customer gets in terms of service and whatever it takes to effectively deliver that output.

James Mwangi: To us, customer service is delivering what the customer wants in the style and in the manner that he likes. We have to find out what the customer needs, and then look at the distribution of the product so that it is convenient to the customer.

Is customer service for a financial institution serving poor people any different from that of mainstream banks?

Hoffmann: I think that customer service is important from two points of view. It adds intrinsic value to your institution and either you believe in the dignity of your customers or you don't, and the internal customer relationship should also be based on certain inherent values. And this should, I believe, be no different whatever your clients' income level. It is simply that the level of competition for poor clients has historically not been as intense. But people always underestimate the competition; whether it is from formal or informal institutions, people generally have a choice whether or not to use the product. Even keeping money under the bed can be a better choice. Customer service is providing the product customers want and if you don't, you won't get any customers. Obviously that's one end of the continuum.

But before we realized this at TEBA, there was a period when we thought we had a captive audience in this market. It was part of my job to raise people's awareness that we never have a captive market – people are moving

---

Expert Box 7.1: Mining Lost Clients
One thing that most MFIs do not do enough of is mining their lost clients, at least those who left in good standing. If the organization has adopted a market-led approach, then it is constantly improving its products and services. So MFIs should regularly inform former clients of these improvements in an effort to attract them back. I would also like to see more MFIs analysing the characteristics of defaulters and delinquent clients, as compared to clients with good credit histories, to get a better sense of what markets they should either avoid or at least take greater care with.

Craig Churchill

their accounts all over, some of them go, some come back. You can never be complacent; having that (false) idea can lead to complacency and (negatively) impact on your business. You have to constantly improve your products and your service platform; everyone at the bank needs to understand that growth and survival depend on this.

Cracknell: Jenny is right – customer service is incredibly important and staff need to understand that customer service is about more than just the typical 'smile brigade' HR perspective that emphasizes being nice to the customer. So we have to create a pleasant banking environment, the tellers have to have the right attitude. Now the problem with that approach is that it doesn't place sufficient emphasis on the basic quality of delivery. Are we actually delivering the right product the customers want? Are we delivering it in the right way? You can smile as much as you like and explain the reasons for poor service as often as you can, but good customer service depends on actually correcting the problem. At the Tanzania Post Bank the major issue was that people were in the banking hall for an hour. No amount of smiling can change the fact that you are waiting too long in the banking hall. You have to identify where the road blocks are. It only takes three minutes to go through a pass book, so why do the transactions take one hour? The total service package requires building an efficient and effective delivery system, which is related to both front and back office.

Granted, the 'smile brigade' approach to customer service can be superficial, but aren't staff attitudes an important part of satisfying customers?

Cracknell: The key thing here is to appreciate that financial services are an invisible product. What I mean by 'invisible product' is that we can't see it, we can't touch it, it's intangible, so people react to the tangible elements associated with the financial product and those are: the people, the delivery environment, what the branch looks like. Staff attitudes are central to the way people see and perceive financial services. They are key to customer service. So much so that many people equate the two.

You have to examine your customer service contact point, and work out

---

Expert Box 7.2: Seeking Client Feedback and Retention

When working with loan officers in Latin America on client satisfaction surveys, I learned that this process engenders loyalty of both clients and staff. When clients see changes they have asked for, they feel that they have a say in the institution and tend to stay. Although loans officers initially perceived customer feedback as criticism, eventually they realized how useful the information is for improving their own performance. When both clients and staff are involved in market research, when their opinion is sought in a respectful way, they are empowered - they feel that they can change the institution. They feel that they have a 'voice'.

Monique Cohen

what is important for clients and your own systems at that particular moment. For the delivery of many of the services, speed and efficiency are obviously major goals, but there are other contact points where the staff attitudes are much more important – for example, the customer service desk, management interaction with clients, and loan officer interviews.

You may need guidelines to assist your staff in their dealings with clients, particularly when things go wrong. Service recovery then becomes the major issue – how do we correct this particular error? This is actually a fairly worn text in the formal financial sector and it's an area where microfinance can pick up a lot of lessons that have already been learned.

You have to have the flexibility that I was talking about earlier and the responses to transform some of these things into concrete actions. You're going to be wrong some of the time, and for me I don't really care because you're going to get it right more often than you're going to get it wrong and overall you're going to move forward.

Wright: Another tremendously cost-effective customer service strategy is having people in the front office, on the banking floor, to assist so that people don't have to wait in long lines and the simple things are dealt with very quickly. It just transforms the client experience. There's huge value to being more proactive, to actually interacting with clients.

Schuster: Yeah. The thing we're working on at UMU is not only someone behind the information desk but also someone who's at the door to help anyone who looks confused or has questions. It's a little more proactive than someone just sitting behind a desk.

Wright: So you don't have a bank jammed with frustrated customers who have gone to the wrong place or they can't read or they're not quite sure what to do; it makes a very big difference. We're going to do a costing of it with Equity. James Mwangi is quite sure that the position pays for itself just in terms of reducing the queues and the time involved, irrespective of all that intangible stuff like customer satisfaction.

A lot of this is relatively low cost and simple to do. It's the attention to detail that will keep clients. And in our business in particular, if we are successful in really having a developmental impact, our clients will hopefully grow and will become better and offer better value over time. We know from studies around the world that in the first couple of years you don't make money on microfinance clients in the main because the loan price is too small. That's why this customer service stuff and retention of clients is really just hugely, hugely important.

Maybe I'm being naive, but I think you can begin with just physically re-modelling the branches, getting a system set up which actually allows staff to serve customers rapidly so they're not constantly dealing with fed up customers who have just suffered an hour waiting in a hot bank. Suddenly the customer's saying, 'Well, this is a modern bank, it's listened to us' and it's all positive. Now if the customers are positive, the staff will be more positive.

And you can get a virtuous circle going. Yes, it's difficult – but we've made great progress with Tanzania Postal Bank on this.

Imani Kajula: In terms of customer service we have done a lot, but of course continue to do more. We did staff training in the branches, and set up a communication link between us and customers to provide feedback and make sure that customer complaints get a response. We also numbered all our teller cubicles so that the customer could refer to a teller cubicle number when identifying poor service or good service. To monitor complaints, we started telephone and e-mail contacts, and established a postal address. All this is easily visible in all our branches. We even have set deadlines for replying to customers. For straightforward questions we have written a frequently-asked questions sheet for staff. This has helped us a lot because we do get 5 to 10 calls, and 4 to 8 e-mails daily. Now, our customers know we are listening.

I would surmise that a physically decentralized branch structure may assist in promoting communication between the institution and its clients. Do you think branch accessibility is an important customer service issue?

Mwangi: Equity has a network of 13 branches that are easily accessible for clients. I think all the branches are within walking distance of most of the clients (of that branch). Physical access is important for clients but less for head office because of the regional operation of Equity. Although Kenya is a massive country, the productive region is literally about 25% of the country, and so the focus and concentration is in that region.

Although not a major factor in client satisfaction, we have been doing mobile banking. We have 18 units, purely to enhance the operations of the branch, so it is still tied to the branch. I think it's a major success for three reasons. One, it has helped to decongest the banking hall; two, it has brought in business by taking banking offices to the people who are tempted to consume because of convenience; and three, it has been done sustainably. We charge extra for the service so that it pays for itself.

Felistas Coutinho: James, I learnt something from my tour of Equity yesterday, in terms of customer service – the speed at which you handle your customers and the way you talk to them. It's like everybody is important. But I would say it's easier in a bank where customers go to a central branch than where you have 8 different credit officers going out in different directions. Knowing where they get stuck and how they deliver their services is much more difficult than when they are in a stationary place and close to a manager who can see if something is going wrong.

That's interesting. So you think that a methodology that sends credit officers out to clients is harder to monitor at the level of customer service?

Coutinho: Yes, it is easier to replicate a consistent level of service using a branch-style operation, but this is not what many clients need. Many poor rural clients need to have access within walking distance, and this can often be done by sending credit officers out into the villages where it is not cost-effective to have branch offices. But it might be more challenging to control the service quality and ensure that the same high standards are applied to all clients.

Charles do your clients come to your offices, or do you seek more client contact by going out to them?

Nalyaali: Right now mostly they come to us, but I think that we should look at the beginning point. In our service delivery we actually go out to people. We tell them about ourselves and inform them of the new development; at that point, UMU goes to the people. When they decide to take the loan, they have to come to us. We have always maintained a physical presence where the clients come in to conduct their business. To get out our information, we go to them.

And one thing I must say is that customers are very interested in the personal approach whereby you discuss and agree on the way forward – what would you like, what you think you can do, how much, how did you save that – and when they come up openly then they also give you some kind of guidance as to how to package the product so that it is acceptable to them.

Well, customer service is clearly a huge topic, one offering multiple strategies. Are there any other specific client retention strategies that organizations are using?

Cracknell: IT is actually an extremely important element of customer service because without a good IT system you become hamstrung. You're looking for ledger cards, your process of approvals becomes longer, the queues in the branches grow, your service time increases. Now that may not have mattered 10, 15, 20 years ago when a large number of organizations were at the same level, but increasing computerization has created awareness in the market place of what service levels should be. Customer service standards de facto within the industry have risen as a result of computerization. Unless you respond to that you won't have a market.

Schuster: As David said, I think computerization is obviously a huge step forward. We've enlarged the branches, added more front line staff-time, things like that, but I think computerization is a big thing. The one consistent complaint that we have had is that it takes too much time or it is too crowded, and I think that is mainly because we weren't computerized.

Steinberg: We have also responded to our clients' request for a reduced pricing – we recently dropped our prices, so our annual effective interest rate is about 20% lower now than it was a year and a half ago. We've introduced client incentives, we've got different incentive programmes going at different times of the year, and then we've done staff training in client retention and client and customer service. Those four things together, I believe, are going to have some positive results on client retention.

Coutinho: Yes, we have really worked at reducing costs and I think that we have reached a level where it would be detrimental to reduce them further unless we are increasing our portfolio so that the costs ratio goes down. Increasing our efficiency and how credit officers handle clients will assist with this.

What about client incentives? My own feeling is that many MFIs, especially in Africa, have not used client incentives as extensively or as appropriately as they might. And here I am referring to both financial and non-financial incentives, such as lottery-type schemes I have seen used widely in Indonesia, lowering interest rates and fees for good clients, issuing 'gold' credit cards, etc. Do you use such incentives?

Adie: We have a range of gifts and prizes, such as cell phones, that are given to current clients in good standing every month. We also have a structured client status program, with platinum, gold and silver status awarded to clients in accordance with a system based on repayment rate, loan size and other factors. These programs have worked extremely well for us, particularly the promotion scheme. I am sure they have contributed both to our retention rate – about 70% of our clients take repeat loans – and to bringing in new clients. All things being equal a lot of new customers will choose to come to us rather than to a competitor when they know they have the chance of a serious prize, one worth a few hundred rand or so.[8]

Steinberg: We've introduced a new thing at FINCA Tanzania. Firstly a client retention bonus, which is 20,000 T shillings, or about US$20. So every time a group is re-capped with less than 10% turnover, the clients as a group get 20,000 T shillings in their pocket.

Martin Holtmann: There is always the issue of making it easier for repeat customers to gain access to credit to get bigger loan sizes. We've introduced preferred client status, the Gold Card, so to speak. After a certain number of repeat loans and perfect repayment performance, customers get a card, and then, instead of being analyzed by a loan officer, they go through a credit bureau to access larger loans within certain limits. However, they repay on the same dates, so we still have a fixed installment in place – a kind of a road towards an overdraft without the overdraft risk. This is enormously attractive for the clients because they have more flexibility to respond to new business opportunities. They don't need to repay the whole loan in advance before borrowing another one as is often the case with the more restricted members. So yes, there has been a whole range of activities to differentiate the clients, break down the market a little bit and provide real incentives for good customers to move up in the ranking and then get access to better, and in some cases, cheaper services.

We started this discussion by acknowledging that clients act on perception. That suggests the importance of marketing and advertising as another form of communication between the microfinance institution and its potential customers. How do you achieve this?

Schuster: I think number one is word of mouth. We also go to church meetings, we go door to door, and we talk to people.

Word of mouth?

Schuster: Yes, word of mouth it is very important. People go to where they are treated well and get better products for better prices.

Fabian Kasi: For us, it is through meetings that our account relationship officers talk with the clients on a regular basis. Marketing tools like brochures are also used. In some parts, mass media are used, such as radio and TV.

Hoffmann: To find new business we make visits to local communities to tell them about ourselves, advertise on radio and visit key leadership around our branches. We also run promotional competitions.

Martin, what have been your experiences in Russia with regard to advertising and client communication what worked for you, what didn't?

Holtmann: There are some issues there. One is the old and very fundamental issue of marketing and advertising. When I first arrived in Russia, I came from markets where advertising had never been necessary because there was always such a big market for microfinance – we didn't spend a single dollar on advertising. If it was a good product and we delivered it well, then the clients would just roll in the door because there was enough world of mouth to guarantee that.

To our great dismay we discovered that that was absolutely not the case in Russia where people didn't trust the banks, they didn't want credit, they didn't see any need for borrowing from a formal financial organization. They thought that maybe the organization would report them to the tax authorities for cheating on their taxes, which is what everybody did and does. So all of a sudden, we were forced to think about an effective communication strategy and we tried out a thousand things. We went from delivering printed material personally to the potential clients to advertising via the telephone, where we would call the companies listed in the phone book. That had a response rate of less than one-hundredth of a percent. We did metro advertising in the big cities. It didn't work very well. We found that in some of the regional centres you could purchase television time by running little advertising lines during the ongoing programs. Underneath the film there would always be a little message – "You want a good loan or you need to do business, call the following number". It worked very well in Russia, at least in the early years.

Word of mouth also helped – by the time we had the first 1,000 clients outstanding there was a certain element of reputation that worked in our favour. But that market certainly turned out to be much more demanding in terms of advertising. In fact, we found that most of Eastern Europe was similar. Likewise, people don't like it if you do too much advertising because they will just say, "You have a good product why do you need to advertise it so much?"

Don't you need to tell people that you've got a good product?

Holtmann: You surely do. But now, we advertise the bank more than the product. If you try to do a customer satisfaction survey many of the potential respondents will think you are a KGB spy or someone from the tax office or whatever. There is an enormous level of mistrust. It would be impossible to get people to fill out a questionnaire.

So how did you track client satisfaction levels if it wasn't through questionnaires?

Holtmann: Since it was a new market, the easiest and most fundamental one that I still know – just seeing if they would become repeat customers. Because my own humble opinion is that if a customer keeps coming back to us for the service then at least they can't be dissatisfied.

Well that's assuming that they have a choice, that there is another similar product elsewhere.

Holtmann: Personally, I think that all things being equal an organization with a very high percentage of repeat customers can't be completely off the map. Doing market research can be very expensive, at least it turned out to be very expensive in Russia. I would be inclined to wait another five years until both the customers and the market in terms of competition have become much more sophisticated. At that time for sure we will need to respond and do more systematic research.

If the client doesn't like the service, or the product, is there a channel for communicating that?

Holtmann: To a certain extent it is much easier if you are in an individual lending relationship with the client because the client has a person in the organization, in the bank, who is responsible for him or her. That staff person is the natural outlet for clients to voice dissatisfaction with the interest rate, or with delays in the application or loan disbursement.

It is typically the role of the branch manager to sniff out, to smell these kinds of problems and to have an open door for customers who want to complain, and in fact, at least in the environments that I have worked in, many of them will come to the branch manager who is the natural next contact person if the loan officer can't handle the issue or if the complaint is about the loan officer himself.

In Africa, a lot of people would not complain – they simply wouldn't come back.

Holtmann: That's true, but if I have introduced an incentive scheme for loan officers that links a stable loan portfolio and repeat customers to increases in salary – systematic problems with the product or the delivery process will be fed right back to management because they will cause loan officers to suffer financially. Loan officers will have their tentacles out there with their clients in order to find out what issues are slowing the growth of their portfolios and therefore need to be reported back to Head Office. Such an incentive scheme offers a built-in corrective mechanism.

James, what techniques do you use to engage with clients?

Mwangi: One of the techniques that we now use quite well is communication at the point of sale. For instance, within the branch we use the notice board effectively to communicate the values of the organization, the mission of the organization, what we think the customer should hold us to. In addition, once a quarter, major customers are called and asked how things are going.

The next one is the statement of accounts. Quite a lot of information is at the bottom of the statement – although most of it will be marketing information. At the moment we are also trying to see whether we can communicate using the cell phone. At a particular point in time, messages could be sent automatically to a client's cell phone – when a transaction hits his account, for example. So we are trying to engage the customer as much as possible using all means of communication.

Finally, in our quarterly published accounts, we give the performance of the organization. It takes a full page every quarter to tell the customer how we are progressing, what the profits are, who has borrowed, how much the staff has borrowed, the level of non-performing loans, and what we are doing about it. So you will find there is quite a lot of communication.

You actually tell your clients what your results are?

Mwangi: Yes, a major full page complement in the press, this is what has happened, this is what we are doing with your product account, these are the people who have helped during the year on your Board.

Cracknell: Perhaps I can interrupt here, James. Another communication and marketing tool that Equity has used is the publication of a 20 years supplement, Twenty Years of Equity, in the national newspaper. It was also on the television and extremely high profile. It talked about the strengths within Equity. When the Nakuru branch opened, within a month Equity had thousands of clients and their growth rate went from four or five thousand clients a month to ten to twelve thousand, and that story is still evolving. The public relations around the 20th anniversary were, I think, one of the critical factors behind this massive growth. Again, this shows that the perceptions of the market are important. After all, the one thing we in the microfinance industry don't appreciate enough is that clients and customers act on perception; they don't act on the basis of having done two months' research to work out where they should get their loan from or where they should put their deposit.

Can you prioritize what you think are the most important aspects of communication with clients?

Mwangi: One is to be clear with clients about your charges. It is now the practice in Equity that they have to be stated in the banking hall. The other communication that we find extremely important now is customer information; there is no service involved, we just provide information on the organization. We have found that we can satisfy customers better when they are able to understand; also the service in the banking hall is interrupted less when customers have fewer questions for the people delivering services. We put the latest products in the field on the notice board, if there are changes they will be put on the notice board – we find that is a more effective means of communication.

In South Africa you will often notice a promotional video running in the banking halls. Have you thought about that?

Mwangi: Yes, that is something we have borrowed from TEBA bank and we are in the process of doing a documentary on Equity. The rest of the time we will use the newsletter and board. Internal advertising in banking and information dissemination are very powerful tools.

Nalyaali: Asking clients what they want can be very good marketing in itself.

A less pleasant form of contact with clients occurs in following up on delinquency – how does that affect the relationship you have with them?

Nalyaali: I think it depends on what has gone before. If the relationship was not good, you would have to work hard to recover money from a difficult party, but if the client is good and he has only just been late for one or two days, I think it influences the approach – how forceful, how aggressive you are. If it is a past client, I think it would pay to be kind and ask what happened this time. But if you are aggressive with a client who is late for the first time, then I think you will definitely create a bit of a bad working relationship, because the client might think that you are not human, you are not reasonable, you are not understanding.

You have an excellent portfolio at risk at UMU. Less than 1% PAR over one day – that's world class. How do you think you have achieved this?

Nalyaali: I think it is a combination of factors. One, during the sensitization time we really emphasize that all money from UMU has to be paid back. And we advise that if you are in doubt, then please don't take the money – it must come back. So that is one.

Two, in the processing we make sure that the clients know exactly when they are supposed to pay – because until recently they had to have these passbooks where we write the date when they are supposed to pay. Now, the onus is on that client to make sure that he comes and pays. At least he doesn't say, "Oh I didn't know", or "I forgot". Thirdly, we have a very good loan tracking system. Loan tracking in UMU happens every day, although we have been manual until recently, every day we know who is supposed to pay on that day, and by the end of the day we know who has not paid, and the following day our staff track that person to find out what happened. Now chances are that if he is a good client they will either admit or they come before the field officer goes to his house. But with the bad ones, staff go knowing that it is going to be difficult. At least the manager, the cashiers and every staff at the branch will get to know that so and so has not paid; should they find any of the relatives or whatever they will definitely remind them that he didn't pay. So that way there is a concerted effort from all persons to ensure that this person eventually pays.

How does that go with being a market-led institution? The clients don't like to be reminded that they have got to pay. How do you manage that?

Nalyaali: We meet the needs of the client, but we also expect the client to meet our needs. And that comes in right from the beginning, during sensitization training you say, ok, you need to know that for us to meet your demands and requirements better you must also meet ours, because it cannot be one-way traffic. That is one of the things that we have emphasized – that in order for us to serve them better they also have to follow the rules – they have to do things that will put us in a good position.

Notes

7. East African annual client retention rates can be as low as 30%, and often range between 40% and 75%. See, for example, David Hulme, *Client Drop-outs from East African MFIs*, MicroSave, 1999 and Graham A. N. Wright, 'Optimizing Systems for Clients and the Institution', *Microfinance Systems: Designing Quality Financial Services for the Poor*, Zed Books, London, 2000.
8. US$1 was between South Africa Rand R6.2 and R6.6 during 2004.

KEY POINT SUMMARY

- Client satisfaction is a key factor determining institutional performance because it costs much more to bring in new clients than serve existing ones. Repeat borrowers and mature clients are less risky and more profitable.

- Client retention rates are a strong indicator of customer satisfaction because dissatisfied clients vote with their feet, especially as their options increase with growing competition.

- Customer service is a focus that draws from multiple disciplines including marketing, communication, and IT. Strategies for improving customer service include:
  * fast and efficient service involving both front and back office functions, especially computerization;
  * positive and pleasant staff attitudes especially at key contact points like the customer service desk or loan application interview. However, while staff attitudes significantly influence clients' perception of the institution, no amount of smiling can compensate for bad service;
  * an information desk or person at the door to the banking hall to answer clients' questions can improve the client experience and reduce queues as people are directed to the right place the first time;
  * an effective feedback system that clearly demonstrates to customers that their issues and complaints will get a response; and
  * clear and complete information about the products and all of their costs.

- Incentive systems for both clients and staff can improve client retention.

- Keeping prices low is key to client retention in an increasingly competitive marketplace.

- Surveys, focus groups and one-on-one contact are all effective means of assessing client satisfaction.

- Communication and marketing strategies include the mass media, word of mouth, and branch notice boards and promotional videos.

- Good public relations exercises can vastly enhance public perception and growth.

- Delinquency needs to be sensitively handled in order not to alienate good clients.

CHAPTER 8

Human Resource
Development and Management

"We need to convince staff of the need for a client focus, and train them in the necessary skills. And then we need to follow up to ensure that they use these skills. We could even have rewards, certificates or a staff member of the month, and communicate the success stories of customer service."

Felistas Coutinho

What issues have arisen with staff in your institution – changes in attitudes, approaches to training and re-training, recruiting etc – as you have shifted towards being market-led?

Fabian Kasi: The shift to being market-led requires a phenomenal change in staff attitude right from the gatekeeper to the CEO and the Board. Attitude change is not an easy process. A lot of issues have therefore arisen, including training of staff, communication, and securing buy-in by all staff.

Jenny Hoffmann: I think part of this 'buy in' involves staff understanding the value for money in market research, and also appropriate ways of conducting it. We've been training a core group of our staff to be able to conduct PRA research. We have also had to work at moving the operational and IT staff from a sole emphasis on their specific areas, to understanding how they fit into the business.

Stuart Rutherford: From time to time we have to address an 'NGO' mentality among the staff, and remind them of commercial principles.

Michael McCord: When FINCA Uganda began to expand its product base we recognised the need to teach field staff to sell. Demand for microcredit had been so high that field staff hardly had to work to get new clients, or for the institution to show dramatic growth with our one product. Once we offered an additional product we found that the field staff were not sales people. We responded with extensive training and follow-up on marketing skills, and saw a significant improvement in employees' marketing activities and methods.

But some senior staff had difficulty adapting to working in an innovative institution. After much effort eventually they had to be replaced in a search for innovative management with the skills to lead the market, rather than simply copying the products and services of others.

Paul Segawa: On the positive side, the shift to being market-led has been exciting for the field staff because of the various demands communicated to them by their clients that existing products cannot address. Our staff training has shifted to emphasize customer care skills, although the recruitment process we use has not yet moved to ensuring new staff have, or have the potential to develop, a customer focus.

Rodney Schuster: UMU has always been market-led so there has been very little need for the type of staff adjustment that others have experienced. The primary adjustment has been toward institutionalisation and systematization as the institution has grown. We were almost too market-led in the sense that we would react in a very informal way, which often proved to be successful. But occasionally we wouldn't implement all the changes uniformly at every branch. In effect, we have had to slow down our market approach to make sure the entire institution is on board before we move forward. This has slowed us down a little, but overall it has made our market-led approach more effective throughout the institution.

It seems to be generally acknowledged that UMU has good solid staff by Ugandan standards right through the organization. How did you manage to do that? Do you do anything different from other MFIs?

Schuster: We have always looked at three things: one, intelligence, two, honesty, three, the ability or willingness to work hard. And whether the candidate was a doctor, a lawyer or had nothing to do with banking didn't matter. As long as they were switched on and sharp, we knew they could pick it up quickly.

Have you invested a lot in training?

Schuster: More so now as we have gotten bigger – it's just harder to create uniformity and harder to spend as much individual time with people. It's more like we need people to do a job and we need it done now and I think that's where training is useful.

James Mwangi: Staff training in Equity takes up a very big portion of our budget – last year the training budget was 12 million shillings (approximately US$ 160,000) which is higher than the budget for marketing. A good reason for this is that we have a very young staff with an age average of about 26 and so we believe that we can reap the benefits of training for another 20 years.

Ernest Saina: In addition to formal training, staff need sensitization to what 'market-led' means. Since I have been at the Bank, I really talk to the staff in the various departments about changing the organizational culture to focus on the customer. If the customers were not there, then we would not be there. I know it is difficult to ensure that this is implemented in all departments and at all layers in the Bank. To help achieve this goal, we have a planning

---

Expert Box 8.1: Capacity to Conduct Market Research?
I do believe that, in order to create a more client-friendly institution, staff need to communicate well with clients which includes the capability to conduct market research. When the staff become interested in the market research and marketing process, they are more open to change and can better serve their clients. In addition, I have found that clients perceive loan officers engaged in market research as loan officers who do their job better. When an institution doesn't have marketing knowledge how can we develop it among staff? I am particularly interested in how to get top management who do not come from a client friendly environment, or have not yet felt performance-related pressure to be more responsive to the market, to recognize the value of market research. This is one of the major challenges many MFIs face.

Monique Cohen

---

session towards the end of each year, where all our experienced people come together, and we plan for the next year – including our objectives for the year, how we will reach them, our strategies, etc. Now and then we have some training courses, especially on subjects like customer service for which we have specific programmes. Actually, we have our own training institute, and we have our staff trained there.

David Cracknell: You must invest in training your staff. One of the strengths of Equity has been that, as an incentive, they said okay, if you study and you are successful we will fund all your course fees. If you don't invest in your staff then you don't invest in your institution because at the end of the day your staff are running your institution. A favourite phrase we use is that if you think knowledge is expensive, try ignorance! But while organizations agree with this, in practice they don't always make the actual investments in building capacity.

But in considering training as an investment, you've got to think very carefully about what type of training you need. Beyond training new staff to be good credit officers, you need to incorporate strategic and project management and marketing skills. Some of these skills are best developed through formal courses, some through mentorship, working alongside competent and capable people. These mentors can be external consultants, or experts who take interns. While there are several options, this process of development has to happen.

Market-led microfinance is not a cookie-cutter approach. There is no single way of doing anything. It requires flexibility, and a flexible organization requires multi-skilled staff with minimum competencies. You're probably talking about having to develop many of these things in-house. You're also talking about retaining staff because as they grow and mature within your organization, you don't want to lose them. So your hiring strategies and incentive plans and succession plans all need to change. The whole Human Resources function in a market-led environment becomes much more significant.

Expert Box 8.2: Scale and Management

I think the biggest challenge in getting to scale in commercial microfinance today is not funds, but management, especially high-level management. Different types of commercial institutions have different kinds of managerial problems, but nearly all have serious management constraints. The pool of highly qualified managers for commercial microfinance providers is still very small, while the demand is rapidly growing. Some much-needed efforts are being made to train managers for microfinance, and also to attract experienced financial managers but there is a long way to go. Three kinds of problems can serve as illustrations.

First, when a microcredit organization transforms to a regulated financial intermediary, its owners and governing board must recognize in advance that their institution will be fundamentally changed. Transforming institutions have multiple advantages: they know the microcredit market, they are experienced in collecting micro-loans, and they know how to reach the poor. But they typically know little about voluntary savings and financial intermediation. The newly regulated institution will need to have a much broader range of clients, some with different needs from those of its poor clients. Another basic difference between borrowers and voluntary savers as clients is that the numbers of the former can be limited, but the latter cannot be turned away - which can lead to rapid and largely uncontrollable growth in the institution. All this has to be managed. But many managers of microcredit institutions do not have the financial skills and managerial experience to take responsibility for fast-growing financial intermediaries (and some board members are not competent to oversee the changes needed in the institution). Yet, there is often a reluctance to make the management (and board) make changes that are necessary when the institution becomes regulated - until it is too late for a smooth, effective adjustment to the more difficult demands of operating a financial intermediary.

Second, member-owned institutions, such as financial cooperatives and credit unions, vary widely. Some work well, but others have long histories of poor management and corruption. Some of the latter have been turned around - often with assistance from the World Council of Credit Unions and others. Member-based institutions also have important advantages as microfinance providers. They are experienced in financial intermediation, they know their clients, their members represent a range of income levels, and some member-based organizations have attained wide outreach. But governance and management can be serious problems. It is not easy to make significant changes in institutions where members are owners and owners are borrowers - and where owners may also be managers.

Third, commercial banks that are beginning to enter the microfinance market generally do not know this market (would they enter an unknown upscale market with a similar lack of due diligence?) Banks have numerous advantages for microfinance - among them, their financial and operational experience, technical facilities and skills, management information systems, and branch networks. And they are normally already regulated financial intermediaries. But often their managers do not understand microfinance demand and do not know how to design or price products for low- and lower-middle-income clients, how to collect small loans, or how to train their staff. And they do not know that they do not know. This is not surprising since in large commercial banks, the microfinance division is still too often considered a punishment posting!

Marguerite Robinson

Ben Steinberg: FINCA Tanzania has also conducted customer service training for all staff (even non-credit staff) as well as advanced customer service training. We have also experimented with client retention training to help staff understand why clients stay and why they leave the program. These trainings are intended both to impart knowledge to staff and to change their attitudes. Staff are also trained in marketing on intake. The difficulty is ensuring that staff absorb the training and implement the lessons. In many cases, the staff argue that their difficulty in providing good customer care is not that they have negative attitudes but that other structural problems, such as overwork, are causing the lower performance.

Training existing staff is obviously very important. But hiring staff who will work well within a market-led institution can also be a challenge. Do you have any comments on this?

Cracknell: Yes, I think one of the problems in microfinance organizations is that their managers fail to recruit people who are talented enough. Managers must be willing to pay for these people, and secondly, actually employ people who are bright and talented. In fairness, some of the smaller microfinance programs have an image problem and the better people don't want to work for them. But as an organization becomes more market-led and brings in more customers, its ability to actually attract good staff increases.

Are competent people available in all markets?

Cracknell: Ah, no. In some markets finding competent people is particularly challenging. Tanzania is one of them, although the Tanzania Postal Bank has shown that finding good people is possible. But in general, exceptional individuals are very difficult to find; you almost have to coax them from elsewhere in the banking sector. In South Africa, colour can be an issue. Given the labour laws in South Africa, talented black executives tend to move from company to company as they get better offers, resulting in a very fluid layer of black management. I think there's a huge need to develop greater talent in challenging markets like Tanzania.

Expert Box 8.3: Managers as Entrepreneurs?
Changing the institutional direction, its culture, its products or trying out new products, is risky, and this should best be done by entrepreneurs. Microfinance with a client focus is more like a business than an NGO, yet many MFIs are not run by entrepreneurs. Perhaps the way in which donor funds have supported the industry has not always encouraged entrepreneurs to take the helm. One might say that in funding product-led approaches, donor support is not always oriented to an entrepreneurial market.

Monique Cohen

FINCA Tanzania seems to have recognised the importance of staff development and is making larger investments in hiring as well as in training. Felistas, how have your personnel strategies changed as you have become market-led?

Felistas Coutinho: Well we used to give prospective staff a math test. That was very important. But now we really want those who can express themselves well in interviews, people who are articulate and will be able to communicate well with clients. We do some testing for numerical skills, but I do think that good communication and inter-personal skills should be the focus for new front-line staff. In the training (of current staff) we give special focus to marketing and knowing your competitors, but still it's a big challenge as some people are harder to change than others.

We need to convince staff of the need for a client focus, and train them in the necessary skills. And then we need to follow up to ensure that they use these skills. We could even have rewards, certificates or a staff member of the month, and communicate the success stories of customer service

---

Expert Box 8.4: Enhancing the Field Officer Job

The transition to becoming market-led has the potential to make the field staff job much more interesting. They have an opportunity to learn from their clients and to contribute to the process of constantly improving the products and services. For the right kind of staff, this is much more stimulating than being a credit-delivering robot.

The challenge is that staff actually have to think. In supply-led microfinance, at least in group-lending models, staff acted more as credit administrators than loan officers - if the group met certain preconditions they got a loan, and then a little bit bigger one, and so on. Staff did not need to exert much judgement. The market-led approach means that services will be more customised to individual customer preferences. I am afraid that in some organizations, existing staff are better suited to be administrators and re-training them may not be possible.

Craig Churchill

In my experience, moving beyond paying lip service to really putting people first is extremely difficult. At FINCA Uganda, if you asked any of the staff who's number one, they would say the customer. But in practice it didn't always work like that. Fifty percent of our credit officers were young graduates, about half were male, while a lot of our clients were poor women and middle-aged. So there were gender and age issues, as well as occasional arrogance among graduates. Once you find and develop staff who actually put a client focus into practice, you have to hang on to them. How does FINCA Tanzania intend to retain their staff?

Steinberg: I think we'll have to give them some kind of incentive, incentive-based pay. And if we promote employees who have been with us, I think it's more likely that they'll continue to work and stay with us. Also, we're hiring one supervisor and two loan officers – lease officers – so that if somebody leaves we still have two experienced staff. But we still only have one person during the pilot stage and if that person leaves, we will have a problem.

Mwangi: The way we try to retain staff is by creating an enabling environment for them. The staff we have acquired at Equity are coming from international organizations. Now I would not have expected somebody to leave Shell Oil Refinery, S.A. Breweries or Deloitte to join Equity, but I think we are a very enabling organization for our key people. By this we mean an environment that provides staff with the tools and resources to perform to the level they are able, that staff development is greatly encouraged, that great training resources are available, that staff input into changes in methodology and processes, and in matters that affect them, are listened to. Staff are empowered as much as possible to be able to do the jobs we hire them for.

Even though, historically, salaries at Equity have been slightly below the market rate, we don't lose staff except those we ask to leave because they are not compatible with the culture of the organization. We've observed that staff favour our enabling environment more than higher salaries. So in my consideration, you don't need to offer more money than anywhere else to attract and retain staff.

Expert Box 8.5: Designing an Incentive System
The steps to designing an effective staff incentive scheme are:

1. *Define and clarify the strategic goals of the microfinance institution. Confirm support of senior management and governance structure.*

2. *Analyse culture, clientele, products and processes.*

3. *Define the objectives of the incentive scheme.*

4. *Determine how much the institution is willing to spend (cost-benefit analysis).*

5. *Decide which staff are to be included in the scheme.*

6. *Choose incentive mechanism(s).*

7. *Undertake technical design work.*

8. *Field test.*

9. *Explain the scheme to staff to get buy-in. 10.Monitor implementation and performance of scheme.*

Martin Holtmann

Imani Kajula: Our success with staff retention has been the result of intensive internal marketing to achieve better relationships within the bank. We held training for the core bank staff – I trained the marketing staff who went on to train branch staff and internal customers to enhance relationships, improve corporate understanding and build a spirit of team work. The Bank imported t-shirts for all staff, which they wear on 'casual Fridays'. We also introduced a newsletter for employees to share and learn about whatever is happening in the Bank.

Furthermore, whenever we have a major launch like this new product that we call "Quick-Account", we present it to the staff first before going to the public. They are the first ones to hear the new ads, the first to see the brochures, the posters and all other materials, so they get a sense of ownership of what is going out to the market. They become part and parcel of what is happening in the Bank. We combine this presentation with a small celebration. We have made quite good progress with these approaches to internal marketing.

Staff incentive schemes can improve both efficiency and performance, and serve as a performance monitoring mechanism. Ernest, do you have an incentive scheme at the bank?

Saina: No. We've talked about it, we've talked about performance pay, but we haven't really gotten to it because we believe that it's not a priority at the moment given the other issues we face. But this is something we want to address in the future. We do have an annual performance appraisal system for general performance. And annual raises reflect performance. But we don't have a bonus incentive as such, and our salary structure is not really competitive.

Alphonse Kiwhele: No, we don't either.

Can I ask why that is? Is it that you don't agree with incentive schemes?

Kiwhele: I very much agree, but I think we need somebody to kick-start this. I have brought in a human resource manager who has attended a seminar in this area, and we should have an incentives program in the near future. I believe incentives are good for improving accountability and for better working together.

How do you monitor staff performance?

Mwangi: We have a five-part performance appraisal system for staff that focuses on performance and the understanding of one's job. The assessment and appraisal is a joint effort by both the employee and their immediate supervisor. This system of appraisal is then used to determine training needs, deployment and transfers, promotion and merit increments, and separation, if need be. The staff have a very strong influence on their appraisal in that they complete a section expressing their feelings about the process. That is supplemented by what we call the 360-degree appraisal. Each staff person is not just appraised by his supervisor, but also by his peer group.

But aren't a lot of institutions structured like pyramids?

Mwangi: That is the style that most of the organizations in this country have been landed with. And so we just inherit without challenging. I think one of the reasons why Equity has been slightly different is due to the Board of Directors that we have. They are all young, highly qualified professionals who have tried to create a very enabling environment in the organization.

How important has this culture of openness been in the success of re-engineering Equity to be market-led?

Mwangi: It has been extremely important. Because it's inclusive it has led to a very participatory style. You find that in Equity implementation belongs to all, so there is a very strong sense of belonging and ownership of ideas and concepts, and this carries through because staff believe in what belongs to them.

The current shift to market-led microfinance involves so much change. Do you need to pay attention to the impact change has on the institution?

Mwangi: Equity has been very dynamic in managing change; we recognize that unless you prepare staff, they are not able to cope. One of the books that really helped us in managing Equity is called Who Moved My Cheese. It's a book about adaptation to change and what happens under all these situations. All staff are given this book to read immediately upon employment

---

Expert Box 8.6: Investing in Human Capital

There is still a strong supply of good personnel at high prices, but when the institutions go to the market they cannot get somebody to write without paying 50% more than they ever expected. I've come across many examples of the dilemma in which one is caught, between increasing the cost base and putting the wrong person into a critical position. Yet, I'm optimistic because, with the right investment, over the next 10 - 20 years you could get a whole batch of bright loan officers coming up through the ranks and the bottleneck should ease a little.

To our advantage, we are a young growing industry, which creates opportunities for people who are looking to go places quickly, and I think that makes it quite exciting. But I think we need to look a hell-of-a lot more at human resource development. We need to link up the educational sectors with the private development sector much more than we have in the past. We have curricula, which is clearly being driven by pedagogues - and not related to the productive factors in the economy. And until you've got that connection we won't be developing a human resource base on which African renaissance will be based.

David Ferrand

because we are so dynamic, we know we will keep on moving your cheese, so you need to be prepared. At Equity, one thing we believe is that if things are constant, you don't make change.

Fraud is an issue in some institutions, has it been a problem for you? And if so, is it coming from the clients or from the staff?

Graham Adie: It's mainly external fraud, but we do have a lot of internal fraud as well. We deal with cash. Our front-end people don't earn a huge amount of money, salaries are market-related, but still not a lot to live on, so they steal. We know how they do it and we catch them. Every guy who steals thinks he will succeed. But he doesn't and we catch them because we've got good systems. We have a whistle blowing line, a hot line, we have all those good things and it still happens. One of the biggest problems is staff taking loans via a third party. And we just can't have that because the staff member will collude with a customer and say, "Look, you take the loan, I'll take it up on your behalf". The staff member doesn't take it up on the customer's behalf, the customer gets a bad credit record. We can't have that. It's fraud basically.

And what about on the client's side? False papers?

Adie: No, we get that, but we're quite good at catching them. We have UV lights in all the branches for checking out all the books. We encounter external fraud mainly with bogus identities or pay checks. But we are getting quite good at detecting it. Obviously, as we get good, they get better – it's an ever-evolving dynamic process.

Do you believe that internal communication is important for staff?

Kajula: To enhance internal relationships we have set-up a teleconferencing facility, whereby we can talk to the branches in a one-to-one kind of discussion and they are able to ask and get replies to any questions they have. I also set up what we call mini-stations, which were much appreciated by the branches. Every day we spend 30 minutes discussing problems and other things they would like to share. Whenever they have questions they call me to consult so everything is cleared up quite fast. And every Friday they discuss one aspect of one product – the aim of this is that each and every staff in the branch and everywhere else understands the products the Bank is offering.

Mwangi: Internal communication has been a major factor in the growth of Equity Building Society, from the executive management meetings to visiting branches every month and addressing staff on critical issues. Until maybe three months ago, I knew all the staff by name, but as the organization has grown we have begun losing touch so we have re-focused on this area. The first thing we decided was to create formal structures for communication that will be sustainable even with growth. One of these is the chief executive bulletin that goes out every Friday to report on what has been happening in the organization during that week. The quarterly report conveys institutional performance to the staff. And in the quarterly newsletter, the staff get to air their views, and learn what has happened in the previous three months. They also learn about workshops or training opportunities, and which staff member had babies or got married. You maintain the cohesiveness through this type of communication.

Do you put that together yourself?

Mwangi: No, it is put out by the staff, but the weekly one comes from my office. I do it myself, although I may ask a member of my staff to write on a particular incident and then we put it together. It goes out to staff in the form of a memo. We've just borrowed the idea of an intranet system and we are waiting for further network connectivity, which will make it easier to circulate this newsletter.

KEY POINT SUMMARY

- Staff need to be sensitized to the meaning of 'market-led' and buy in to the transition and the changes it will bring.

- Investing in staff training at multiple levels is a must. Developing staff capacity for market-led, customer-focused microfinance requires a variety of training methods including formal courses, internships and mentoring.

- Post-training, managers need to monitor the extent to which staff actually embrace a client-centred approach and use the skills they are taught.

- Hiring strategies also need to change – qualities such as innovation and adaptability become more important than mathematical skills.

- Staff retention strategies become ever more important given the significant investments in hiring and training. These include salary incentive schemes, an enabling environment and healthy internal communication.

- An enabling environment can compensate for less-than-market-rate salaries. In such an environment, the staff members have opportunities for training and advancement, their opinions are heard, they are informed about the institution and have a sense of belonging and ownership of its innovations.

- Channels of internal communication are important for a sense of staff cohesiveness. Weekly bulletins from the Executive Director's office, daily conference calls with branch managers, and monthly newsletters are tools that market-led institutions have found to be effective.

- Performance appraisal can be an effective staff development tool – particularly if they are inclusive.

- Staff need to be able to cope with change if the organization is going to be truly dynamic in its growth.

CHAPTER 9

The Institution
Capacity, Structure and Governance

"…the whole organizational structure determines to what extent you can be market-led It starts at the top. If the top is not market-oriented then the organization will never become market-led. But if you have a structure that drives the process from the very top with involvement in the critical areas of the business, it is easier to achieve a market orientation."

James Mwangi

What progress has your organization made towards becoming more market-led? What has this involved in terms of organizational design, systems, strategic thinking, practicalities, and so on?

Peter Simms: Credit Indemnity still has a way to go to become market-led. Over the years, we've had one product essentially, a four-month loan, which we've probably offered for about 24 years. For many of those years the focus was on developing systems to keep costs down, taking it from a ledger-based system in one branch to a computer-based system at 23 branches. This has worked for us and facilitated profitable growth. Our process was to multiply branches which was relatively easy because everything was so system driven. Open a branch, train staff, set up a system and off they go. We only needed a manager to make sure everything happened, that all the boxes were ticked. This phenomenal organic growth was not matched by product development. The only significant product development was developing the market profile.

Fabian Kasi: Actually, a lot has been done to ensure that FINCA Uganda becomes more market-led. A marketing section has been instituted; the regional office has hired a marketing specialist who is assisting us to design marketing procedures and enforce a marketing approach to all operations; a tool has been put in place to measure customer satisfaction on a regular basis and a customer care charter is being developed. Our corporate image has also been enhanced with corporate colours, letterheads, visual materials, marketing tools, brochures and so on.

David Cracknell: This type of corporate branding is very much an evolving agenda for MicroSave. We're interested in how corporate branding impacts client perceptions of infrastructure and quality of service. A strong brand incorporates both, and leads to customer expectations. It becomes much easier to identify deviations from the norm, and where things are not as they should be. Branding sets up a series of promises, if you like, to the customer, 'This is how we will behave.'

Corporate branding in East Africa tends to concentrate on the physical aspect of the environment – the logos, the colour scheme, the flooring, the ceilings, and the physical infrastructure. And yet, the less tangible aspects, which are very important in the South African financial industry of brand personality, are really not expressed here very well.

Paul Segawa: As Fabian said, FINCA Uganda has made some progress with both corporate branding and market research. While we now have a marketing department and the product development process, not all the other systems have changed. For example, we seek to provide product features that the MIS can support, not the other way round. We also have problems in responding to the client needs that we identify because the whole product development process takes a long time. The response time doesn't indicate that we are very keen on meeting our clients' needs. However, currently we have developed a couple of tools that aim to capture information on client satisfaction. We've developed what we call a client satisfaction analysis, which is based on information we gather from our suggestion box on clients' issues. Hopefully down the road we shall analyse that information and make the necessary changes. But we have not yet really used this ... it's only one or two months old.

Alphonse Kiwhele: We started pursuing a market-led approach back in 1999 when we adopted a new strategic plan that was written as a result of our market analysis. We analyzed all aspects of our business, in terms of the external environment, internal weaknesses, opportunities and threats; we surveyed the various players in the market, comparing their strengths as against ours, and at the end of the process we came up with a strategic plan outlining our vision, mission, goals, and objectives. We then narrowed down the kind of activities that we have to perform during the planning period, and to achieve these activities, we sought strategic partners such as MicroSave.

I would say we are now more or less about 60% along, in terms of the MicroSave objectives that we set ourselves in terms of savings products generally, I think we have made very good headway.

Expert Box 9.1: Know Your Market
You cannot truly help an institution that is not designed in such a way that it is able to react to a market. One thing that I have learned is that if you don't clearly understand your market then you can't even start to design the operational structure of your institution. How can you do this if you don't know what you are aiming for? And this is of course the client, the market, through specific products.

Gerhard Coetzee

Stuart Rutherford: At SafeSave, we have constant ongoing discussion and modification of product design and delivery methods, fed by research into the financial service behaviour and preferences of the poor. This is not a shift in SafeSave's case – SafeSave has always attempted to provide what it thinks the market prefers despite the difficulty and expense. SafeSave has support for its approach from the Board, although the Board is not yet a key participant in service design.

Getting an organization to be market-led involves a lot more than rolling out a product. What other things need to be in place to make sure that the product is going to work?

Segawa: FINCA's key product has been significantly supply-driven. 'It was, "This is what we have, so let's sell it out there". Now, as FINCA wants to be a market-led institution, it has to go through a significant cultural change, or strategic change, in that we need to start building our strategies based not on what we have to sell but on having established a potential market. That change has started, and will need to go through the entire institution. It doesn't stop at just the product champion.

FINCA also needs to appreciate the whole concept of customer satisfaction, and invest resources in it. The management team will also have to accept the fact that the initial investments in information gathering and redesigning, how we do things may not produce immediate benefits. We've been stuck in the past on these issues, but I think we are now making good progress. We are starting to look at marketing-related expenses as investments rather than costs. And the changing strategic thinking of the institution at the country level is also happening at the international headquarters. So for this investment in marketing to take place, we as an institution have to be willing to say, "Okay, lets transform the institution, restructure and change how it goes forward.'

Rodney Schuster: Yes, that transformation to a demand-driven institution really takes commitment at all levels. UMU is different in that I think we have been committed to this since our inception. As we have become a larger and more complex institution we have had to institutionalize some of these market-led tendencies. The major adjustment has been the division of the company into two divisions. One division deals with the daily running of operations while the other division concentrates on strategic planning and research and development. But our best staff is in charge of research and development. And I think that shows the commitment. That's how important we think it is.

Felistas Coutinho: I think the first big step we took at FINCA Tanzania was hiring a marketing officer. When she first came on board we were throwing literally everything to her. Then we realized that it was too much, so we got two others, one for each region, with her as the supervisor, and there is still too much work. We have also incorporated customer service into our evaluation. We made a suggestion box available to our customers, which we didn't have before. We open them up weekly, make sure to follow up on their suggestions. We are developing more marketing materials and training staff every year in customer service. The first year they get basic customer service, the second year advanced customer service, the third year, relationships. So we keep on upgrading.

Ben Steinberg: In the process of learning how to conduct client surveys most effectively, the question quickly changed from, "How is it that we need a marketing department?" to "How did we survive without one?" The information, outreach, communication and plans have become critical factors in FINCA Tanzania's success.

Jenny Hoffmann: TEBA has also allocated financial and human resources to market research. There is still a tendency to focus more on the technology and operational issues around providing a product rather than keeping the focus on the demand, but this is improving over time. However it has led to a revision of the product development and project management process and real attempts to provide measurements for customer satisfaction levels and other input.

James Mwangi: It is about survival. I think that if Equity had not changed there is a question of whether it could have managed to survive, and if it had, whether it could have experienced the same level of growth both in volume of business and profitability that it has experienced. Our exponential growth has been driven by the change in approach to become a market-led organization.

Equity Building Society can by many measures be considered a leading example of a market-led microfinance institution. I don't think that getting there was easy. What have been the biggest obstacles in achieving it?

Mwangi: One of the obstacles has been the changing of mindset. By this I mean that people have their own way of doing things and when you are saying you want to be a market-led organization, then the culture of the organization has to change. The transformation process will challenge the way things have been done, and because this involves change, you need to be patient to see the results.

You have to do research to clearly understand the customer and her needs. Your company must be able to respond both to what you learn about your clients, and to what you don't yet know about them. It means finding out how your company needs to change to be in line with clients. How should your institution look if it is to be client-led? What are the best investments you can make? This is when your company has successfully transformed. But it's a major, major challenge.

Ernest Saina: For us, the issues are do we have the products to meet customer needs, the systems to support those products and the vehicles to grow the business? A big, big problem on which we are spending huge amounts of money and resources has been on our systems, especially on the MIS. In 1999, we began to replace our outdated computer system, but unfortunately the bank started on the wrong foot, with the wrong selection of banking software, the wrong consultants, and so forth, and the whole process eventually failed. It has been re-started now and we are moving forward slowly but surely. The computerization of our systems and of our operations is really crucial for us to be able to handle 1.6 million customers. Another big, big headache right now is the congestion in the banking hall; the way we operate doesn't really lend itself to acceptable customer service, or delivery of our services.

How important is the nature and type of organizational structure to a microfinance institution's focus on clients? Some practitioners seem to think it is critical, others less so.

Saina: You have to have a proper structure, you have to have the right people within that structure, or you are not going to be able to perform what you have set yourself to do. We went through structural review about a year ago, and I think we have a structure now that will enable us to become more responsive to our target group within the market.

Mwangi: I think I agree with you. The whole organizational structure determines to what extent you can be market-led. It starts at the top. If the top is not market oriented, then the organization will never become market-led. But if you have a structure that drives the process from the very top with involvement in the critical areas of the business, it is easier to achieve a market orientation. Equity is a very open organization – they feed all information across the board, both vertical and horizontal. It's not just a free flow, but also a fairly open, flexible, collapsible structure. You find the Board will be involved in most of the customer activities and they are literally involved.

Expert Box 9.2: A Demonstration Effect

Let me come back to why we as donors work with the retail institutions. We don't believe that we can seriously work with enough institutions to create the capacity needed. I think that would be extraordinarily naïve. But what we can do is build demonstration institutions. I think it is absolutely fundamental, and I think that we've already seen signs of success here where you are getting more and more commercial-type players interested in what were once core microfinance markets. But you can't stop once the institution reaches self-sufficiency. We can demonstrate that this game matters, which explains why we work with an organization like Equity. The key demonstration effect there is you can actually build ultimately their ambition is pretty clear – a national microfinance bank. That needs to be demonstrated.

David Ferrand

I think one of our strengths – and we hope we will not lose this – is that Equity has a very simplistic organizational structure, which is very thin at the very top and very wide at the bottom. The bottom has direct access to the very top, so the bureaucracy is not there and all of the top is driving all segments of the organization. You find that the directors – the managing director, the human resource director, the operational director – all have clear responsibilities, so there is no question of conflict between the departments.

Cracknell: I don't think there is one ideal structure, because I think structures change over time and they change as the institution matures. As institutions move towards becoming market-led, they build new competencies into their organization. Early in its life cycle, a microfinance programme is unlikely to have skills in marketing and market research. But a fundamental shift occurs when an institution begins to put the customer first. It is more concerned about the speed of its systems, and the flexibility of its service delivery. This transformation creates tension between the new marketing functions and the old operations functions. This point of tension within the institution requires very creative management and it's frequently a point of stress, but in a sense it is the driver of market-led microfinance.

Beyond competency in market research, marketing and customer service, the transformation to a market-led institution will also require new levels of competency in finance, particularly product costing, responsibility accounting, corporate centre accounting, and branch accounting. MFIs will have to examine cost structures. Without an efficient delivery mechanism your ability to service more rural communities will be limited. Risk management will also become more important as will treasury management and liquidity management.

In a market-led organization, I would expect to see greater but selective use of consultants in key critical areas where the institution may need to test the water. For example, an institution may bring in marketing skills on a consultancy basis before employing a marketing manager. Institutions need to understand the value of a particular function to them before they can make that very significant investment in money, in resources, and they need to have information on which to make that decision.

But is that going to make them more market-led?

Cracknell: No, but it will make them more profitable and increased profitability and efficiency enables one to deliver more products to more people; that in itself is market-led. To manage the transformation challenge is like juggling balls. The ability to juggle, to manage multiple products, multiple initiatives at the same time is actually fairly critical in the transformation process.

How does the organizational structure change with growth?

Mwangi: This is one of the greatest challenges, which we have just started to work on, so we are not sure how well we will perform. We have brought in a new structure, with good open channels of communication in order to maintain close relationships. As the structure grows, the needs of the shoulder and the neck and the head will also grow substantially, but whoever is at the top will have to balance control with close relationships. If Equity can pass that test, it's headed to be a great organization.

Capital has also been a major constraint for Equity Building Society. Why? Because, the organization has been growing faster in terms of volume than the capital base. Although we have adopted a very conservative policy and retain almost all profits, we are not generating sufficient capital growth. So, we have been looking for a possible investor who can take up a bit of shareholding and equity, and we have been lucky – it looks like AfriCap is considering becoming an equity investor.

Kiwhele: Capitalization has been one of our main institutional issues too. Our strategy now is to come up with the measures that can lead to privatization so that we can get the capital we need: when you are private you can also find funders to finance various programmes. Currently our capital is about US$1 million which is not enough because even the IT is already costing that much. At this time we are allowed to borrow, provided we get the approval of the central bank, the Reserve Bank.

David, what role does leadership play in the transformation to market-led microfinance?

Cracknell: Leadership is key. Equity, for example, has a dynamism personified by James Mwangi. Fortunately, he is not the only leader, but he drives the process. He's had a very clear picture of what he wants to achieve, and that vision is incredibly important. What our strongest action research partners, TEBA and Equity in particular, have in common is a very strong vision. It enables them to target their transformation process.

While James has been critical in this initial phase of the transformation at Equity Building Society, he will be less so in the next phase. I don't think you can achieve full transformation with a single person.

There's a lot that comes from having the right people in the right places. A unique feature of Credit Indemnity is that it has incredible depth in its management team – between 12 and 15 people who are really strong and competent, all working in the same direction.

Expert Box 9.3: Success Rests with the Management and Board
Success depends on management who understand the business, and understand the reality of developing financial services. Thinking about different institutions I've worked with, success is tied to the inclination of management, the people who have to implement decisions. I think 70% of the success is derived from management's drive...and the Boards you have.

Gerhard Coetzee

What about governance, why is governance important?

Graham Adie: I think that governance is exceptionally important, because at the end of the day it is not just the formal issues such as clear vision and mission that set the direction the organization will follow, it is about integrity. The leadership – the Board and management – set the tone, the honesty and integrity with which everyone, from all parts of the organization, embrace in their goals and objectives and ultimately determine the relationship with clients. A strong governing ethic founded on integrity makes a huge, huge difference.

What practical measures can one take to promote good governance?

Adie: One of the powerful things at Credit Indemnity was good governance on an informal basis. It's a lot more formal now, but to start with the integrity of the leaders was huge. Taking advantage of company vehicles, company petrol and little things like that let standards slip; it is extremely important to avoid that. If your top people are not behaving in the most impeccable fashion, you can't expect your lower end guys to do it. Our top people wear uniforms. I wear the same uniform and I am governed by the same rules as the most junior echelon of staff member. And for me that is fine. If I go somewhere, I don't travel first class, nobody does, and nobody complains. Because you can say if the top blokes are doing it, you also do it. These are the issues that I think lead to a healthy business environment. And those are the type of governance issues that I think are very important in a business.

How then do you get to an appropriate level of accountability and integrity in the governance structure?

Adie: It has to come from the leadership. Without the high standards of integrity and behaviour among the leadership, you can't do it. I can't stress good old-fashioned integrity enough. Objective measurements are extremely difficult, and to be a proper decent manager you have got to have good judgement. I think what is important as well, very important, is for managers to simply rely on listening to people to staff and clients and suppliers and technical advisors and consultant, listen to everyone and synthesize. You get so many managers who think they know absolutely everything, and become autocratic.

Cracknell: In organizations with strong management, the governors ration what the organization does, identifying and focusing on its priorities. But in organizations that have grown very quickly as a result of market-led growth, you tend to find that the Board of Directors doesn't grow commensurately in competence, capability and capacities. You need to evolve your Board as you evolve your organization and management. Ideally management should look at its Board as a strategic resource and if it isn't, an opportunity is being lost. But of course it can be very difficult for a Board of Directors to evolve because

> **Expert Box 9.4: Principles of Good Governance**
> *The characteristic of bad governance in some respect is the very fact that it is not looked at until a crisis point is reached. What are the characteristics of good governance? There is no right or wrong. There's a temptation to take a very simplistic view, and this is where some of the expectations get very high, particularly in cases of privatization...a very simplistic but Friedman-like belief is that the responsibility of the governance is to the company's shareholders, to ensure that their interests are faithfully represented, and these, in some quarters are assumed to be about maximizing profits.*
>
> *Yet, the business of microfinance is embedded within a wider context and people who are working in the industry have a much more holistic sense about it. I suppose you could say that at the next level up, we would be talking about representing the wider interests of the institution, looking at the long-term sustainability of the organization in addition to short-term profit streams. But balancing those interests, being the sort of nexus of those interests within the organization is hugely complex and difficult and requires a continuous process of decision-making, all of which are probably contestable from the stakeholders' perspective. So, it's not going to be very easy to find a simple governing principle. I mean no doubt there are checklists or things that boards do which might be indicative of good governance, they would be proxies though of the fundamental issue of accountability to stakeholders.*
>
> **David Ferrand**

they're notionally recruited at an annual general meeting and very often the management of the organization plants them.

The question of course is, how can governance of microfinance be improved?

Martin Holtmann: There is talk outside the microfinance industry – which I would support inside our industry as well – to ask Directors to put a personal nominal stake into the organization, even if that stake is lent to them by the organization that they represent. I personally think that that model should be tried out to change this awful situation where you have a lot of people sitting on the Board who are representing other people's money – and in microfinance this money is often grant money or nominal equity investments that are basically a fig leaf for grant money. Let Directors of MFIs cough up $20,000 or some other meaningful sum of personal money or debt that they own in the case of failure and let's see how they change their behaviour. I would actually expect that many people would then choose not to sit on Boards any more.

Cracknell: Boards need good information, the right amount and type of information. Jenny Hoffmann achieves this in TEBA by creating a Board information pack that is sent out before Board meetings.

Another strategy for improving governance is to ensure that directors know their rights, responsibilities and duties. Equity has begun to take its Board on a retreat for a couple of days every year which allows much greater quality of interaction with the Board than is possible during a short meeting, especially in an organization that is expanding and changing as rapidly as Equity. In a market-led institution, the nature of governance may have to change which will require that you place greater emphasis on increasing the level of understanding of your governors and regularly updating it.

A third strategy is to rotate new people onto the Board, which offers management an opportunity to expand the competencies of the Board.

Improving accountability among executive managers and governors is critical. The Board of Directors needs to be empowered to govern, to put the brakes on, or to actually remove management when necessary. This can be very difficult because most often the Board is removing the person who appointed them in the first place. So you have your first conflict of interest. You know, it's very difficult to bite the hand that feeds you. Finally, I think that remote governance is a problem. FINCA is a case. You can't have remote control governors, or Board members, it simply does not work. Successful governance has its hands on the beast, local hands on local beasts. Remote governance may not be able to prevent poor management from impacting upon the organization until far too late.

Do you find that your Boards understand and support a shift towards becoming market-led?

Steinberg: Yes, our Board has recognized that the market is becoming more competitive and that we have to respond more quickly and effectively both to market opportunities and market threats. The Board is regularly updated on marketing activities at Board meetings. We have also discussed problems with some systems (e.g. adapting the IT system) at Board meetings. We are in agreement that marketing is key to FINCA Tanzania's future. But we have made the case to the Board usually in terms of competition rather than philosophy – which is kind of an indirect way of talking about being demand driven.

Hoffmann: Our Board's concern is that the bank should make a developmental impact and therefore must meet the needs of the targeted customer. There is no conflict. I think there is an assumption that a customer focus is there unless they hear that it isn't. They're more concerned about risk management; they see that as their major role.

Schuster: UMU's Board has always been supportive of our efforts to be market-led. The Board has seen market-led microfinance as the most effective way forward since our inception. We have like-minded people who have similar vision. I mean, I don't think I could handle trying to convince them at every meeting that we want to do a new product. I've never had that problem in six years. Never. We say what we want to do, and how we want to do it. Obviously they have questions, but usually these are about how to make it work, and the implications – the risk management. And that's totally different than having to try and convince people.

I think if we didn't give them the audited accounts, they would ask. If we didn't talk to them they would wonder why. I think we have a really unique Board situation in the sense that I probably talk to one of the non-executive Board Members at least once or twice a week, and Charles, the other executive Director, does as well.

So communication is very important?

Schuster: It's incredibly important and very high priority. You just could not – it would be so awkward not to have talked to one of them, or not to give them something, or whatever for a long period of time.

Simms: Communication is always important, and communication with your Board is really important. The investment that you make in your Board management is an investment that might give you the best return you can get.

A lot of Board members – volunteer Board members if you like – of many MFIs or NGOs don't have the time to maintain a high level of involvement. Rodney, what's different about your non-executive Board members?

Schuster: I guess the only answer I can give is to go back to how we chose our really critical Board members. They were good friends of Charles, both of them; one's a lawyer and one's an accountant. So when we first started it was just Charles and I, and when we had legal issues we would see Willie, and he would give us a lot of time, even though he's a very busy guy. He would spend a half-hour, an hour, answering legal questions and also very interested in what we are doing, how we are doing it, why we're doing it, how things are going. Whenever we wanted as long as he was free from work, he was ready to see us. That was amazing. And also with our chairman, Mr. Kasbanti, it is the same thing but this time, accounting questions. He came to our first branch you know an hour and half to two-hour drive on a bad road just to come and see it open.

And so basically when we were saying we needed to form a Board after about six months, Charles didn't suggest them because he felt he would be biased. I said what about those two and he said, 'Yeah, I definitely agree'. So it was essentially people who were committed and willing to work, and give us time.

KEY POINT SUMMARY

- The transformation to a market-led institution must have the support of the entire organization, starting at the top.

- Successful leaders in market-led microfinance are often guided by a strong vision.

- Good governance is founded on, and infused with, integrity. Leaders need to be role models for their staff.

- The introduction of new skill sets should occur gradually, often starting with market research, marketing and customer service. The establishment of marketing departments has been an important shift for many of the microfinance institutions. As the process develops, transforming institutions will upgrade competency in finance, costing, and information technology.

- Necessary investments in system upgrades, new staff positions or staff training will mean additional costs that may not bring immediate benefits.

- A market-led corporate culture introduces new elements to MFIs including improved customer service and corporate branding.

- Good internal communication among the Board, management and staff will help to cultivate and maintain a focus on becoming a market-led institution.

- The transformation to market-led microfinance may require change at multiple levels of the organization, including the Board. Management needs to cultivate the Board's endorsement of market-led microfinance with improved, strategic communication and education.

- The skills and resources a Board of Directors brings to the organization may need upgrading for a successful transformation.

CHAPTER 10

The Environment

*"I think in our case in Uganda, the legal environment has not affected us at all –
it has been neutral. But I think the economic environment has been significantly
positive. There are so many people who have come to set up small businesses."*

Paul Segawa

**What role has the environment – economic, social, regulatory, supervisory
– played in either supporting or detracting from a market-led approach
for your institution?**

Stuart Rutherford: SafeSave specifically responds to conditions in the densely
packed slums of Dhaka, and we are conscious that its way of doing things is
seen by its clients as contrasting with the Bangladesh MFI standard product,
which dominates the scene here. Lack of an MFI law makes it difficult to
orient SafeSave around deposit-taking – as this is the essence of the service
(daily visits from a deposit-taker). Not being able to intermediate is a serious
impediment to service design, and generally keeps us in a box where all
clients must be loan-eligible, which doesn't reflect the composition of the
market. For example, we have difficulty making a savings product for very
poor people sustainable because we can't intermediate the funds to others.
There is a big market for that product.

James Mwangi: I don't think there is anything unique about Kenya that
has ideally contributed to the success of Equity. It is a country that has been
growing at an almost negative growth rate in the last 15 years, and has been
in recession for nine. Yet, interestingly, the organization has continued to
grow at the rate of 50 to 60% over that same period. The investment in the
market and nationalization of the market deliberation might have had a
positive impact on the growth of Equity Building Society.

The factors that we could consider negative in Kenya have not all had
negative outcomes. These include political instability, particularly with the
succession of elections, the prolonged depression, and the suspension of
donor support. These have not had any negative effect on Equity. Why not?
I'm not really sure – we have simply worked very hard to give our clients what
they want, even while making mistakes in the process, and this has worked
well for us. Perhaps not letting outside things interfere has been helpful.
Equity is a regulated institution supervised by Central Bank like any other
commercial bank, so it is a member of the deposit protection fund and here I
think that the regulatory authority has been a positive influence. The Central

> **Expert Box 10.1: Good Regulation Supports Market-led Microfinance over the Longer Term**
>
> *Appropriate regulations can be enormously important in running the institution in the long term. Ultimately, bank regulators want to see the manager of the bank run the institution in a way which is going to impact the long-term interests of the depositors. And ultimately, the mantra that we keep coming up with, that we should be advocates of market-led microfinance, is about being in business for the long term. That's the future. There's no way you are going to stay alive in a competitive market unless you are market driven.*
>
> *But there is a negative aspect and that is the weakness in the regulatory system in many countries. I think that the reason we have seen so many scandals over the last two decades has more to do with governance than technical capacity. That is a point worth emphasizing. I think that supervision is much more difficult. I don't think we have the right legal framework that combines a lightness of touch with substance.*
>
> **David Ferrand**

Bank of Kenya has supported Equity and in most cases has consulted with us as opposed to just enforcing regulations, because they like what is happening to the organization.

Ernest Saina: It is somewhat different for us as Kenya Post Office Savings Bank is a para-statal, subject to government direction, and all the expectations of a para-statal. I'll give you an example. We have a staff of around 1,300, when maybe 1,000 is logically what we need. But if we were to go to a retrenchment programme, we are unlikely to get support from the government because we are putting more people on the ground, and we do not have the funds to carry a retrenchment programme. We would have to go to the government to fund that, and we are unlikely to get support for it. So we have said, "OK we've got to ensure all employment for strategic positions, and you don't replace anybody". But private concerns like Equity can decide to restructure and retrench without notice.

Also, we would like to be in a position to offer our customers a full range of financial products but we are not allowed to do lending. You know right now, I think our customers are getting a raw deal. From time to time they need to borrow to meet cash flow requirements, but we are not able to help them. We have made a proposal to the government and the Central Bank, but in Kenya we have had a bad experience with a third of the banks, especially government-owned banks. The government has a lot of bad memories. We have been pushing it and last year the Minister of Finance at that time accepted and said, "Yes, you need to do that and the next time parliament resumes we will put it through". Now there has been a change of government and we have to get it passed with the new minister. This is a legal issue we want to be able to achieve in the next year.

Ben Steinberg: FINCA Tanzania is not yet regulated/supervised by the Bank of Tanzania (although this is due to change). However, in terms of economics, Tanzania is still transitioning from a socialist system to a market-led one, and there are enormous opportunities for financial services in the low-income markets. While the demand is enormous, the supply remains quite limited. Recognition of the potential rewards has spurred the market-led approach in Tanzania. With that said, there are some limitations. Tanzania, for instance, does not yet have a credit reference or a national ID system, making it extremely hard to identify individual credit histories. This increases the risk for lending activities, particularly those that are individual as opposed to group-based. The social environment in Tanzania is quite supportive as our clients are very expressive about their needs and demands. Our task is to act on their recommendations and to do so more quickly.

Paul Segawa: I think in our case in Uganda, the legal environment has not affected us at all – it has been neutral. But I think the economic environment has been significantly positive. There are so many people who have come to set up small businesses.

Schuster: At our inception, the environment was not really supportive. Most players in the Ugandan market thought that UMU's market-led approach was destined to fail. Things like flexibility, customer service, and innovative loan products were considered nice concepts, but something that could not be implemented in a sustainable manner in the developing world context. While most players were neither supportive nor a hindrance, donors were hesitant to fund UMU in part because of our market-led approach.

David Cracknell: I think environment does have an impact on being 'market-led'. The general banking environment sets the standards against which organizations are competing and against which they can attract clients. We have already discussed how the competitive environment, or lack thereof, has a significant impact. In Tanzania, you can come in with a much lower quality offering to the market place and still get a lot of clients through your door because you're still better than the competition. The opposite is true in Uganda. There, a huge number of ATMs have been launched into the market place and are taking the upper level of the low-income market by storm. There's huge competition in that market.

Expert Box 10.2: The Risk of Regulation

Perhaps one of the biggest challenges to becoming market-led is the potential negative role that some regulators, apex institutions and donors play in perpetuating the replication of supply-driven models, and not allowing MFIs the flexibility to try new approaches – this is particularly a problem among wholesale lenders that have strict criteria designed to limit their credit risk, but which ultimately inhibit innovation.

Craig Churchill

Expert Box 10.3: Microfinance in Africa and Asia – Similarities and Differences

The differences between Africa and Asia seem readily apparent. Asia has 37 countries with 61%, and Africa has 54 countries with 13%, of the total world population. Asia has some of the world's biggest and most populated countries and urban centres, while Africa has smaller and less densely populated countries. Africa generally has less dependable rainfall than much of Asia and relatively poor infrastructure. As a result, Asian MFIs have the opportunity to reach more rural communities and to achieve truly massive scale Asia is home to almost all the MFIs with over 1 million clients: BRI, BRAC, ASA, Grameen Bank etc.Conversely, African MFIs are typically focused on urban areas and the asurrounding countryside.The average size of Asian MFIs reporting to the MIX[1] was 12 times bigger than those reporting from Africa. CGAP estimated in early 2004 that 528 million clients were served by MFIs in Asia and 25 million clients were served by MFIs[2] in Africa.[3]

Furthermore, the cost of living in most parts of Africa is markedly higher than in Asia, and because of the lower population levels there (in absolute terms) fewer professionals are available for recruitment into the microfinance sector. These two factors mean that operating expenses and particularly the salaries paid in the microfinance sector in Africa are typically higher than those in Asia. As a result, the MFIs in Africa tend to make larger average loans per borrower and target people significantly less poor than in Asia. In addition, the cost of financial services in terms of interest rates charged on loans as well as fees for savings services provided tends to be markedly higher in Africa. These high value loans at high cost are necessary to cover the current operating expenses in Africa, which are more than double those in Asia.

However, some of these important differences decrease significantly when the 4 large Asian MFIs (averaging 1.3 million borrowers) are compared with the 6 'large' African MFIs (averaging 30,000 borrowers). While the large Asian MFIs still lend significantly further down market, the Yield on Gross Portfolio (real) are broadly similar (Africa: 29.8% and Asia 32.9%) as are the Adjusted Operating Expense Ratios (Africa: 10.6% and Asia: 9.1%). It is only in the Operating Expense/Loan Portfolio ratio where another difference arises (Africa 21.4% and Asia: 15.5%). The resultant Financial Self Sufficiency ratios are almost the same for Asia (130%) as for Africa (133%). This disaggregated analysis of the larger MFIs suggests that there are considerable opportunities for further improving the economies of scope and scale in medium/small African MFIs.

Another striking similarity is emerging in microfinance: it is increasingly clear that throughout the world poor people are willing to form groups to access services but that they prefer individual services. In Africa group methodologies are being gradually replaced by individual lending, a trend that is also taking place in the Asia. The implications of this for the cost structures in Asia remain to be seen.

Finally, it is also clear that the formal commercial sector is entering (or in many cases has entered) the microfinance market in both Africa and Asia particularly on the savings side. This trend, coupled with the growing recognition of the important role played by Postal Banks and Agricultural Development

> *Banks in the low-income market (and the potential for enhancing their services), means that another "microfinance revolution" is in the air. And as competition increases in several of the markets in Africa and Asia, we can hope to see more customer responsive products and delivered in a more efficient, cost-effective and market-led manner to the benefit of clients and the financial institutions that serve them.*
>
> **Graham Wright**
>
> 1. *The MIX is the Microfinance Information eXchange: www.mixmarket.org*
> 2. *MFIs as traditionally defined, not including the Postal Banks, Agricultural Development Banks etc. - see the MIX's MBB for a detailed listing of the MFIs reporting to it.*
> 3. *CGAP presentation "Global Trends in Microfinance" April, 2004.*

And of course, the regulatory environment is key, especially as regards savings. Many microfinance institutions don't have the regulatory power to collect savings. Having said that, the mass market for saving services is very often in the postal banks and organizations like Equity Building Society that do have the appropriate regulatory authority. The question is whether the Central Bank, under a regulatory structure, is going to be able to influence NGOs and other microfinance institutions in a positive way, and that's a big question mark.

Martin Holtmann: Regulation and supervision are difficult topics I think. Talk about regulation of finance organizations has been the flavour of the last few years. I think it's vastly over-rated in terms of its impact on the industry. In some cases, regulation can stifle, for example, where the minimum capital requirements for converting to a bank have been fixed at such high levels that it becomes economically unfeasible to actually go ahead. If you need to cough up $20 million just to operate a microfinance bank in Colombia, then by definition you will choose to stay an NGO. And where regulation blends with supervision, even the best regulation will not help if supervision is weak. Following the standard banking model to supervise microfinance organizations can have very bad consequences for them. For instance, this might require a 100% provision on all loans the moment they go out the door because they are uncollateralized. Yet, the issue that I am much more worried about is that most supervisory authorities lack the tools, the personnel, and the wherewithal to actually be effective supervisors. And thus, we have created a monster because we regulate certain types of organizations anyway. We've created a market and the public sector is not able to supervise this market the way it should. Sometimes I think we would have been better off if we hadn't gone into this regulation in the first place, and just let a thousand flowers bloom or grow.

Most microfinance clients that I know of, at least while they have been saving with small NGOs or co-operatives or whatever, are perfectly aware of the fact that their money is at risk. Some of the research by MicroSave and others has shown that people actually know that there is a certain default risk of the financial organization they are dealing with.

A central reason governments regulate savings is to protect the public, especially poor consumers, and in many cases this is supported by some form of deposit insurance. How important do think deposit insurance is for microfinance institutions?

Holtmann: Of course many developed markets have it. The problem is that someone needs to fund the scheme which ultimately penalizes the good and successful organizations, and provides an advantage to those who might not be so good. But I am also worried about the moral hazards aspect because once management knows that deposits are insured, they might be tempted to do more risky business on the assets side. So again I don't think deposit insurance is the panacea or the kind of thing that will change the industry fundamentally. It may work in some countries, it may not work in others.

What is the regulatory situation like in South Africa?

Graham Adie: Firstly, the government policy is to look very closely at their lenders, but this is a double-edged sword. Clearly South Africa has seen large-scale abuse – reckless and predatory lending. The MSRC has now introduced a national loans register, and is sending outside auditors to look at a lot of loans, to see whether your lending has been reckless in other words, can the guy afford to pay back the loan? Now in principle, that is solid because you shouldn't over lend, but there are several problems. The first one is regulating reckless lending. How do you define it? And how do you deal with it when a lot of the people are accessing loans through those employed in the formal sector – which is really the only place you can get a loan in South Africa now. It is a big issue. The second is, as we all know, that the rates in South Africa are tremendously high, and people are making super profits. There's no doubt about it. There will be downward pressure on rates, probably from the market, but perhaps legislative pressure as well. If the government can make legislation to suddenly cap rates fairly aggressively, and they do it on short notice, we could be in a lot of trouble. We might not be able to adapt quickly enough. That's why we tried to dramatically cut our costs, so that if such legislation does come, we will be in a better position to handle it.

I think that with micro-lending in South Africa, the big cost is still the cost of capital, assets to grow your book. It creates barriers to entry and increases the cost of doing the business. This is the problem that the government faces, because it has to be seen as intervening to stop malpractice. But the more they regulate, the more expensive it becomes to do the business. You know, we have a National Loans Register where everybody has to subscribe, you have to send your data on every single loan – the borrower's name, address, ID number, the date and amount of the loan, and the repayments. While practitioners have access to that data and find it useful, we also have to pay for it. Registration fees at every outlet is R700 per year. I mean it costs us about R160,000 a year to be a member of the MSRC. And the other thing is, given its problems so far, most of the practitioners don't respect the integrity of the data. Not everyone is sending their data like they should, and because it is still new, it's not delivering at the moment.

Jenny Hoffmann: An issue for us is that the current restrictions in South Africa around the exemption to the Usury Act loans mean that we are not able to design loan products that fulfil real client needs. An example is small business owners who require overdraft facility-type products. The costs of small loans for amounts above the Usury Act exemption limit of R10,000 also make it difficult to provide these products for housing and small business. The new anti- money laundering acts also make it much harder for us to open accounts for our targeted clients who often do not have a formal address or use public utilities, even though the money laundering risks of servicing this segment must be low.

Unfortunately, economic success for business in an area depends as much on the available infrastructure as the finance. Unfortunately, lack of co-ordination persists between local government and the private sector around this.

Imani, how has the banking environment in Tanzania influenced the Tanzania Postal Bank's decisions to introduce market-focused changes?

Imani Kajula: First of all, I must say that the whole financial banking industry in Tanzania is currently undergoing massive competition and re-engineering. The market trend in the country is to enter the regional markets. Secondly, the advent of multinational banks has brought new standards of banking into the country – good banking halls, good services, well-branded outlets. Together these developments called for re-engineering of the Postal Bank strategy. We decided to upgrade the IT system, which should support the introduction of modern products, and the microfinance product. Another new strategy is to provide services across the country – retail service I mean. In my role as Chief of Marketing, I have to set a strategy to take the Bank where it rolls. Basically the Tanzania Postal Bank is government- owned, but now it is undergoing the privatization process. What I found among the market is that – the image of the bank, I could say, was quite low; most people confused the Tanzanian Postal Bank and the Tanzanian Post Corporation because once upon a time they were one organization. However, in 1992 the government decided to split it into three entities – the Tanzanian Postal Bank, Tanzanian Post Corporation and Tanzanian Telecommunications.

So what did you do to differentiate the Tanzanian Postal Bank from the competition?

Kajula: I set up four units within the marketing department. One is the product development and management unit – because although we had a lot of products, we were not managing them, and eventually some needed re-packaging, to be restructured and so on and so forth. Second was the issue of internal marketing and public relations, because the relationships and internal communication within the bank, between departments, was

---

Expert Box 10.4: Industry Leaders

It is widely recognized that commercial microfinance is the only possible route to meeting demand from the hundreds of millions of people who lack access to financial services today. As happens in any emerging industry, a relatively few large industry leaders have begun to dominate the microfinance markets of their respective countries. This is occurring now in all major regions of the developing world (but to different degrees in different countries). Industry leaders – found among many institutional types - typically share a common set of characteristics. They are generally large, mature, well-governed and well-managed, regulated financial institutions with clear ownership structure and considerable assets. They are externally rated, commercially funded, and financially self-sufficient. Technical expertise and appropriate management information systems are priorities. And they have wide outreach through well-developed branch networks or federations of member-owned financial cooperatives. Industry leaders typically maintain a corporate culture highlighting institutional accountability and transparency, knowledge of the microfinance market, efficiency, high-quality staff training, and performance-based incentives. Not all leading microfinance providers have achieved all these traits, but most share most of them. The characteristics these institutions hold in common also include large market shares in their respective countries - shares that reflect an outreach that is wide and deep.

What is being captured here is a moment that occurs in all emerging industries. A relatively few well-governed and well-managed institutions providing commercial microfinance become industry leaders and gain substantial market share. But the weaker institutions persist for some time. Eventually they join the ranks of industry leaders, find small special niches, merge or develop strategic alliances with other institutions, change orientation, or close down. Commercial microfinance is not an end. It is a process. I think that in the coming 50 years or so, it will have disappeared from most parts of the world. And for the first time in history, microfinance will have become an integral part of the financial sector.

Marguerite Robinson

---

quite poor. Lack of staff knowledge about bank products and programs led to poor service delivery. That is why I created a special section to deal with internal marketing and added the public relations. Furthermore, the bank wasn't taking care of its customers with specific people to handle customer complaints or staff training in customer service. So I set up a marketing unit which will be doing customer service for the bank. The last one is promotion and advertising. The bank had quite a good number of products but they were not known in the market. So I had to set those four major sub-sections in the marketing department.

HIV/AIDS is a major external environmental issue that affects all microfinance institutions in Africa. How large an impact do you think is AIDS having on your institution, and on the sector generally?

Hoffmann: The incidence of AIDS obviously makes it hard to provide the term and value of loans that the market would like, given the risk of the breadwinner falling sick.

Adie: There are two direct issues for us on AIDS – the customers and the staff. At the moment, AIDS deaths are not an issue at all. We have less than 1% per annum of our customers dying. So it's not a lot.

And the impact of AIDS on your staff?

Adie: While I am not aware staff having died from AIDS it is beginning to become an issue when people in the branch get sick and everyone grows concerned for them, both the people around them and here at head office. Our management team is still working out our policies. There are disclosure issues – some don't want to disclose their status so you can't deal with it. This also affects morale – you can try and help the person if you know the status, but you can't if you don't.

Cracknell: I think there are multiple impacts. Our study of the impact of HIV/AIDS revealed different issues at different points in the disease cycle. At the early stage of the illness, people are working, but their productivity is lower because of opportunistic infections. So they lose working days and income but spend more on medical care. But the actual impact on the family is slightly lower. The bed-ridden phase of the illness is very expensive. What people do and how they cope varies by location; where the social taboo of AIDS is greater, the refusal to acknowledge it means that people will go further to treat opportunistic illnesses, will spend much more money, and will push themselves further into poverty as a result. The financial stress at this stage is huge. Then, when the breadwinners die, children have to be absorbed into other parts of the extended family. This has placed much greater pressure on families in relation to the costs of raising children. There are ways in which financial institutions can respond by developing new products and services related to school fees. But potentially it also means that institutions are shy of developing longer-term loan products and so you tend to see a gap in the market in terms of longer-term loans.

Ultimately, AIDS will decrease market size, decrease productivity in the market place and, I'm guessing, will massively decrease savings mobilization in families that have been hit by the illness.

Expert Box 10.5: The Loss of Human Resources
We don't hear enough about the impacts of AIDS on the industry; the biggest single constraint on development in the so-called finance sector in Kenya or Africa, I would say is human resources. You can buy everything else, but in the end, human resources make businesses. And when you are potentially losing people – leaving aside the humanitarian disaster - the business disaster is that you have invested a huge amount of money in an individual.
David Ferrand

Holtmann: When we first went to the Rakai District with Centenary Bank we had numbers that had been collected by others indicating that about I don't remember the exact percentage – but about 40% of the adult population in the Rakai District were HIV positive. We subsequently decided to substantially reduce our loan term compared to what we were offering in the typical branch setting. Also, there may be very good ways – and I think some people are experimenting with this already – to link insurance with lending to ensure that at least the loan is repaid in full.

And yes of course, HIV/AIDS also has an impact on staffing. On an average, sub-Saharan Africans need to train – without being scientific about it – three times the number of staff that others train, because it is just a very sad fact that many staff members will pass away. And they tend to be the younger ones more often than the older ones. That has a big cost in terms of training – apart from all the other suffering and disturbance of operations that happen when a staff members dies. But it certainly means, especially in Uganda, we tended to take in twice the number of new staff than we would have in a similar operation in say Eastern Europe or in America, because AIDS in not such a big problem there.

KEY POINT SUMMARY

- Many environmental factors, such as the extent and nature of competition, government regulation, and the HIV/AIDS pandemic, all have an impact on the microfinance sector.

- Negative factors, such as political instability and economic recession, however don't necessarily hinder the growth of microfinance institutions, especially those that are meeting client needs.

- Para-statal financial institutions like the Post Office Savings Banks do not have the same freedom and flexibility to respond to the business environment as private institutions do. The dictates of commercial business may be at odds with government policy or political climate.

- The regulatory environment influences product offerings, particularly with respect to savings.

- While improved regulation is recognized for fostering industry standards and sustainable microfinance, questions remain about the regulatory capacity and sensitivity to the unique services, products and methods of microfinance.

- The incidence of AIDS will probably have an increasingly significant impact on the nature and type of products, such as the term and value of the loans offered, and on the size of the market.

CHAPTER 11

Critical Issues

"I think it does boil down to having the vision to deliver an effective, efficient service and having the system to be able to do that. So vision, management, and systems have all been crucial and I think if you don't have these three building blocks you're simply not going to deliver a large number of services to low-income clients."

David Cracknell

What do you believe to be the most critical issues for institutions in becoming market-led and client-focused?

Michael McCord: I think market research is the most critical, because without it, the institution does not know what the market wants. This forms the core of the product development process and from it springs products that are more likely to be successful in the market. But it is also important not to lose sight of the demands of the institution. It can be too easy to focus strictly on the market to the detriment of profitability and institutional stability. The market-led approach must always be balanced against the needs of the institution and what the institution can and should reasonably provide. The market can lead us, but we should not always go.

Jenny Hoffmann: Also, ensuring that every staff member – front and back office – understands and acts on this imperative.

Fabian Kasi: Yes it involves changing the attitude of staff, right from the gatekeeper to the Board.

Hoffmann: Other important issues for us are improving our time to market

---

Expert Box 11.1: Top Three Picks
1. *Understanding client preferences, and recognising that this is a constant process.*
2. *Hiring, training, motivating and maintaining staff who can think, innovate, and contribute to the constant improvement of the organization.*
3. *The risk of product proliferation: being market-led does not mean that MFIs need to offer 10 different financial services; this creates marketing problems, confusion, and management problems. Instead, find the three to five most important services and allow them to be adapted to various purposes.*

Craig Churchill

through better planning and processes, and improved information flows and analysis.

Paul Segawa: For FINCA Uganda, the whole approach to strategic planning has to change to put the customer on top, because one of our current strategies for product development is to import various FINCA experiences from elsewhere and implant them in the Ugandan market.

The second thing is enhancing the marketing function through capacity building to transform the entire institution; to appreciate the need to be market-driven and to transfer the skills needed to really focus on the market. Of course, another critical issue is the information system as this is going to provide us with a mechanism for monitoring whether we are achieving our objective of being market-led or not. Right now, we don't have something of that nature so it would be hard to tell whether we are actually getting there or not.

David – you would have a good sense of what the critical issues are from the work that you do with MicroSave's action research partners.

David Cracknell: Yes, management, flexibility and responsiveness. Strong, experienced leadership needs to have the ability to take a decision and to run with it, backed up by appropriate IT systems. Inflexible IT systems have forced pilot tests to come to a grinding halt while systems-related issues are resolved. I would also put communication up there as a critical issue.

Communication with staff or communication with clients?

Cracknell: Both. Without good communication you can have the best systems but no action; you don't develop the information you need to manage the transformation process to become a market-led institution. We have seen failures of communication consistently within MicroSave. Every single institution had problems when it failed to communicate changes in policy. The best institutions have formal and structured communication channels and they also have a strong corporate culture which encourages indirect communications, which guides people to what is right for the institution and what is wrong. This enables people on the ground to make decisions.

The transformation process requires appropriate competencies in place, and these will vary by situation. Organizations need to respond to needs as they evolve.

What have you found to be the three most common success factors among your partner microfinance institutions?

Cracknell: I think the first has to be the clear vision of the management. This is true even in a bureaucratic organization like Tanzania Postal Bank. TPB, TEBA and Equity all have a clear vision that the organization is going to grow, serve more people, and serve them efficiently and effectively. A strong management commitment to the vision drives through the organization. I think that's the first point.

The second point in all three organizations is an increasing commitment to marketing. All three have invested in building their capacity in this area.

I think a third factor that underlies success is the IT systems. In the case of Equity, the IT system is allowing them to offer a quick, fast, efficient service. TEBA is beginning to pilot-test debit cards with new banking software. TPB has networked eight of their branches and they're beginning to find that they can serve a lot more people.

That's on the Equinox System?

Cracknell: Yes, and they've been able to service another 9,000 or so accounts in the last month. I think it does boil down to having the vision to deliver an effective, efficient service with the system to accomplish that goal. So vision, management, and systems have all been crucial. And I think if you don't have these three building blocks you're simply not going to deliver a large number of services to low-income clients. Systems are incredibly important because you are producing a high volume of transactions at the low margin so you need to control costs. Now, that may well be possible using manual systems in Asia where there are clients at your doorstep, but it's much more challenging in the African environment.

Charles – do you have a good idea of what the key factors have been in UMU's success?

Charles Nalyaali: That's a tough one. One area that I definitely think is key to having a successful demand-led organization is the management, especially the top management. I will just explain a little. UMU is in a very strategic situation with its management. We have two senior executives who come from different backgrounds but are working together to ensure the best possible institution. So you have Rodney who has come from America bringing plenty of choices and things like that, so he is market driven, and then you have Charles who is local, he knows the local environment, he knows what people really want and how they want it, and also how they should be treated and all those kind of things. A combination of these two has really helped us to identify and be in a position to provide the kind of services that the client would need.

We have also developed a good middle management. These branch managers have trained on the job, basically seeing what we see and how we do it. They replicate wherever they go, and it has really worked very well. In addition, we have been quite aggressive in taking advantage of the opportunities that avail themselves to us. Opportunities among the staff, the clients, and the funders.

I must state we have been, can I say lucky, in that right from the beginning we were properly funded, and our association with the Central Bank gave us credibility. Thirdly, I would say that the market economics have been good. The environment in the country has been positive for economic development.

Felistas Coutinho: I think one is the staff attitude. Having them on board, knowing that the customer is very important, and being committed to giving them the best service. Two is having an MIS that is very supportive and I think the third is product development.

I think we've also got to be aware of what is out there, of the competition. The other thing for FINCA is having the loan capital, the money to expand. Since we don't have grants any more, and we are borrowing commercially, it's a challenge for us because the commercial banks aren't yet sure whether we are creditworthy or not!

Is there anything else that you think – lessons learnt from FINCA Tanzania, that would be of interest to anybody else?

Coutinho: I don't know if it has come out indirectly, but I think having an empowered staff is very, very important if you are going to go out and deliver a good service. Sometime back in FINCA we believed in micro managing, but that's detrimental if you want to deliver customer service. You've got to give people some power to be able to do that. You have to be flexible. So I think empowering the staff is something that is critical if you are going to be customer driven.

Maybe the other lesson that I have learned is that new staff need time to learn, which means that new people are costly. And the speed at which you handle customers is very important. Customer feedback is very important.

Ben Steinberg: I would say first develop marketing capacity. The second thing is follow a good process for product development that's inclusive and integrated. The more people participate in the process, the more successful the new products will be. We made a mistake when we changed our interest rate and started charging an up-front fee. We went from a 5% flat to 5% up front and 3% effective monthly, which was an error because it was a top-down decision. When MicroSave brought in the market research we realized that we had solved some old problems, but created a lot of new ones. And I think making sure your management team understands the importance of being client-led is another important factor.

Are you saying that people are the most important factor?

Steinberg: The process is flexible, but if there is no commitment or capacity, nothing is going to happen.

What do others see as the challenges or critical issues for their institutions?

Ernest Saina: The critical issues for product development and delivery? Firstly there must be a demand for each product. Secondly, the product should actually be able to contribute to your profits. The biggest problem that we have faced in getting products out into the market is lack of profit.

And what would be a third one? The systems must be in place for the delivery of the product. Although we had a proper process for the development of the product, when we started rolling it out we found we had a systems problem and a lot of expenses. This is an area I am very cautious about with a new product. You must have all your systems.

Alphonse Kiwhele: For us there are some big challenges. Let me name several. The first one I would say is IT. This is the number-one priority that we are trying to address, so that we can be more competitive and continue to grow our share of the market.

The second thing is capacity building within the organization because you can have very good systems, you can have good communication channels, but if you don't have the manpower to support the system you may not achieve your targets and objectives, so building your human resources is very, very important.

The other challenge I think is the question of capitalization of the bank. I think the Tanzanian Postal Bank was established with a very small capital base. As we expand, we need to finance the networking, the IT systems including the banking software, and data banking software in order to remain in the market. Yet, it is the government's policy in Tanzania to pull out from not only running but also owning shares in the Post Bank. So our strategy now is to try to come up with measures that can lead to privatization so that we can finance our various programmes.

The capital of the bank is currently about US$ 1 million but the IT and the banking software already cost about that much.

Expert Box 11.2: Another Top-three List

The first thing is that we definitely need to look at two sides of the coin in terms of the market/client/product mix and determine the carrying capacity of the market, the strength of the demand for our product, and how it will affect institutional sustainability.

Second is staff: the quality of your staff, your deputy staff, the training you put into your staff. How do we provide them with guided, on-the-job, real experience. We make a mistake in believing that we can train our staff outside the context in which they must work.

The third key factor is related to product and product design in response to the market. Those are the three things.

Gerhard Coetzee

James Mwangi: I will tell you what I believe to be the three most critical areas. The first one is product development itself, getting the right product. The next one is the right technology to deliver the product. The speed of the delivery will be determined to a great extent by the technology adopted. Then there is the staff that have to be chosen and the culture acceded to by the staff.

Peter Simms: One of the most critical things for us to focus on is our IT system. It's extremely powerful, but it's very rigid, very difficult because its so systems driven. We need to change the system to make it more sensible and able to adapt to our products.

KEY POINT SUMMARY

The most critical issues for success as a market-led institution include the following:

- Market research and a commitment to marketing.

- Staff training and getting all staff 'on board'.

- Flexible, reliable and speedy management information systems (IT).

- The leadership and depth of the management team.

- The ability to be flexible and responsive to the market.

- Communication with both staff and clients.

- A clear vision that pervades the organization.

- Good middle management.

- Innovative product development.

- Adequate capitalization.

CHAPTER 12

Conclusion

The growing interest in market-let microfinance is being driven by two forces: the marketplace and what it takes to thrive there, and the industry's overarching aim to improve economic and social welfare of the poor through access to financial services. In the marketplace, increased competition and declining levels of client retention have led to reduced operating margins. Microfinance institutions are responding to their evolving markets with measures that are bringing them back to their original starting point – their clients. To protect and expand market share, they are focused increasingly on responding to clients' needs – through more appropriate products, faster, more convenient service delivery and competitive pricing.

Understanding and then meeting client needs are two sides of the same coin. Internal institutional constraints that limit the capacity of the MFI to deliver desired services are often the key impediment in meeting client needs. Leading microfinance institutions consequently place much emphasis not only on understanding clients' needs and desires, but also on building internal capacity and responsiveness. This encompasses all aspects of the business. A focus on attaining best-practice management and governance of the microfinance institution, investing in staff, and accessing appropriate technical assistance whenever available are critical, and clearly have been central to the successes of the leading microfinance institutions. It is only through serious efforts to overcome these internally derived limitations, that microfinance institutions will be able to genuinely serve the needs of their clients.

An enhanced ability to meet clients' needs should, of course, enable a microfinance institution to be profitable. But, such client-centered responses are also bound to improve the social returns that are the moral foundation of the industry. At this point in time, industry leaders understand that a shift in approach, a fundamental change in the way business is done, is necessary to achieve both the financial and social returns that make microfinance such a powerful, compelling tool in the fight against poverty. Seen as serving these dual goals, the commercialization of microfinance is not 'anti-poor' as some have contended; rather, the same commercial principles that have historically driven traditional business to 'put clients first' are being harnessed to guide MFIs to more appropriately and sustainably serve the needs of their clients.

The conversations in the preceding chapters clearly illustrate both the opportunities and the vast array of challenges that microfinance institutions face as they become truly market-driven. For me, one of the key lessons to be learnt from this discussion is the need for the whole institution to focus on understanding and meeting client needs. The practitioners I spoke to have gradually come to understand the magnitude of this task and the resulting need to pursue a methodical and structured approach to achieving it. The leading microfinance institutions place much emphasis on building internal capacity and responsiveness, encompassing all aspects of the business. The conversations in this book reveal both how far institutions have come in re-educating their staff and revamping their operations and how far they have yet to go. These conversations also help us understand that the process of transformation is, by the nature of its magnitude, gradual. And by the nature of the marketplace, ever evolving.

That many practitioners have overcome the myriad obstacles with a sense of optimism and continued belief in the ability of microfinance to help the poor overcome adversity, and to assist them in their climb out of poverty, should renew all of our own hopes for the future. It is only by overcoming the challenges facing our institutions that the microfinance sector will be able to meet the immense demand for financial services that exists among the poor. And in doing so we who believe that microfinance is one of the best tools available in the fight against poverty, can collectively make a significant impact on the lives of the hundreds of millions of poor people who still lack access to appropriate financial services.

About *MicroSave*

Reaching the huge untapped market for microfinance entails building the capacity of financial institutions to innovate to meet the diverse and changing needs of a broad range of poor clients. In short, a market-led approach. *MicroSave* is at the forefront of efforts to move microfinance from a product-driven to a market-led basis. Market-led microfinance optimizes product development, product delivery systems, customer service strategies and corporate brand & identity.

Benefits accrue to the financial institution by enhancing customer loyalty, reducing drop-outs, and increasing profitability. For the clients, more appropriate, customer-responsive financial services allow them to better manage their household finances to improve their lives.

MicroSave's Research Programme

MicroSave has already completed over 80 action-oriented, operations research studies and 20 case studies on a wide variety of topics including clients' needs and behaviour, reasons for clients leaving MFI programmes, strategic marketing for financial institutions, staff incentive schemes, product costing and pricing, the product development process, institution and product risk analysis etc.
Many of these issues are summarized in 50 two-page Briefing Notes.

MicroSave's Action Research Partners and Toolkits
MicroSave works primarily in Asia and Africa with carefully selected financial institutions (including postal savings banks, commercial banks, non bank financial institutions and NGO-MFIs) to assist them to deliver market-led financial services to the low-income market. Using the toolkits it has developed, *MicroSave* provides training and technical assistance to its Action Research Partners on:

1. Strategic Marketing for MicroFinance Institutions
2. Market Research for MicroFinance
3. Costing and Pricing of Financial Services
4. Process Mapping
5. Institutional and Product Risk Analysis
6. Product Marketing Strategy
7. Planning, Conducting and Monitoring Pilot-Tests
8. Product Roll-out
9. Staff Incentive Schemes Development
10. Customer Service
11. Corporate Brand and Identity

12.   Strategic Business Planning
13.   Human Resource Management
14.   Individual Lending
15.   Delinquency Management
16.   Loan Portfolio Audit

MicroSave's role is to ensure that its Action Research Partners have an adequate understanding of the issues involved in moving from product design to full scale implementation.

MicroSave's Capacity Development Programme

The *MicroSave* toolkits are comprehensive and, in most cases, relatively easy to use without training. However, many consultants have found significant value-added in receiving formal training and experiential learning through practice-based courses offered by *MicroSave* and its Certified Service Providers (CSPs)/trainers (to locate a CSP visit the *MicroSave* website www.MicroSave. org). *MicroSave* has developed training curricula for its suite of toolkits (outlined above) and uses two approaches to develop capacity to use these:

1.   The Young Executive Professionals programme, which provides field-based learning opportunities within *MicroSave*; and

2.   The Senior Service Providers programme, which provides focused, practice-based training on the *MicroSave* toolkits to senior microfinance professionals.

More on *MicroSave*'s research programme, toolkits and capacity development programme is available from www.MicroSave.org

MicroSave
Market-led solutions for financial services